# NAKED *at the* HELM

# NAKED
## *at the*
# HELM

### INDEPENDENCE AND INTIMACY
### IN THE SECOND HALF OF LIFE

by
# SUZANNE SPECTOR

SHE WRITES PRESS

Published 2022
Printed in the United States of America
Print ISBN: 978-1-64742-085-7
E-ISBN: 978-1-64742-086-4
Library of Congress Control Number: 2022902826

For information, address:
She Writes Press
1569 Solano Ave #546
Berkeley, CA 94707

She Writes Press is a division of SparkPoint Studio, LLC.

*Book design by Stacey Aaronson*

*To my parents*
*Helene and Emil Mogul*
*and my brother*
*Malcolm Mogul*
*with deepest gratitude and loving memory*

*"This process of the good life is not, I am convinced, a life for the faint-hearted. It involves the stretching and growing, of becoming more and more of one's potentialities. It involves the courage to be. It means launching oneself fully into the stream of life."*

CARL ROGERS
*On Becoming a Person*

# CONTENTS

# PART III
## MY 60s: EXPLORING

# PART IV
## MY 70s: BEING

# PART V
## MY 80s: CELEBRATING

# PART I

———

## My 40s
## STRIPPING

# THE COUCH CRUNCH

March 1976

*Picture this: An imposing white house with dark green shutters sitting elegantly atop a patchy snow-covered hill. At the bottom of the long, snakelike driveway, a budding forsythia bush is readying to burst forth in the golden fury of early spring. But above, the top of the driveway is blocked by a massive rusting black metal dumpster. And from a third-floor window of the stately abode, stuffed brown paper bags are flying through the air, straight into the bin, one after another, like basketballs through a hoop.*

Never having been a successful athlete, I was ecstatic. Heave-ho. I raised each bag up to the window, then sent it soaring into the bin, scoring every time. Heave-ho. I released bag after bag filled with the old mail my soon-to-be ex-husband, Myles, had left on countertops, tabletops, and desktops all over the house. And heave-ho, I dumped all of his parents' stuff that he'd insisted on taking when they died.

3

I felt cleansed. Now I could put the house on the market and find a simple, smaller place for my three girls and myself. Splitting the money from the sale would be the carrot to get Myles to finally sign the divorce papers; after two spectacular business failures, he desperately needed the money.

When the garbage truck arrived to pick up the bin, I asked the guys to top the load with the ratty old couch from our first apartment that had been sitting in the garage for years. *Thunk,* the couch landed. And then, the ultimate, delicious satisfaction: The truck backed up to the bin, reached out its metal arms, grabbed that dumpster, and flipped it over. With a resounding crunch, the couch was pulverized, along with all the other garbage left from my marriage.

Moving out of this grand old house might have looked like downward mobility, but it felt liberating. I had just turned forty, and I was unburdened. No more marriage. No more big house. No more Myles.

I paid the dumpster guys, then sat down at the picnic table to savor the moment. The couch crunch felt almost orgasmic—a gigantic release from years of sexual frustration and swallowed rage. I lit a cigarette, took a deep breath all the way down to my hungry crotch, and thought back to the beginning, almost eighteen years earlier.

## Fall 1958

Like most girls coming of age in the 1950s, I had a fantasy of domestic bliss. What that meant exactly, I wasn't sure. I knew I wanted a husband who was smart and independent, a self-starter like my dad. And I knew I wanted to be a loving, relaxed, easygoing wife, not a tense, overcommitted career woman like my mom. In my marriage, I wanted passion and romance—and at least a bit of tenderness.

When Myles and I returned from our honeymoon in the summer of 1958, he went to work as the sales manager for his father's electronics importing company. I "played house" for a few weeks in our new apartment on Eighteenth Street in Manhattan, and then returned to Columbia University and Mount Sinai Hospital for the second year of my master's degree program in social work.

Each night before bed, I chose a different nightgown from my closet full of beautiful, new, enticingly touchable sleepwear. For all twenty-two years of my life, my mother had insisted on serviceable cotton pj's—no nylon baby dolls for me. Now, the sheer black gown with the lace bust beckoned seductively in my closet. But I couldn't garner the courage to slither into it, especially on a weeknight. Instead, I chose a silky blue gown with straps that slipped right off my shoulders with the slightest shrug. I felt ready to be ravished and went into the bathroom to insert my diaphragm. When I came back out, Myles had already turned off his lamp. I climbed into our queen-size bed and slid over to his side to cuddle up. He let me stay there, in the crook of his arm, my head on his shoulder, while we chatted for a little while, but then he said, "I'm tired. Time to go to sleep." When he took his arm back and turned away, I tried to calm myself, tentatively spooning around his back, but I was too shy to reach out. *Wasn't the man supposed to initiate sex?* I didn't dare try. As tears welled up inside me, I dashed into the bathroom, closed the door, and sobbed with a towel over my mouth, trying to silence the voice in my head that repeatedly asked, *Why won't you touch me? Myles, I'm here. I want to be held. Stroked. What's wrong with me? Why don't you want me?*

I wished I had a girlfriend with whom I could talk about sex, but after seventh-grade kissing games, my girlfriends and I had stopped sharing details. Nobody talked about sex. I wondered what my friends' marriages were like. Did any of them fall asleep crying too? Or were they having sex all the time? Who else could I talk to? Certainly not my proper mother. So, I made an appointment with Dr. Schneider, our family psychiatrist.

In his office on the Upper West Side, I was relieved when he invited me to sit across from him at his dark wood desk—no Freudian lying on the couch. I tried to describe my relationship with my husband.

"I love Myles. I think he loves me too, but I don't understand what happened. When we were first dating, last year, his hands were all over me. We ended up at his apartment all the time. I gave up my 'pretend virginity' pretty quickly, and the sex was great."

Dr. Schneider didn't seem shocked at my brazenness. He nodded benignly, so I continued.

"But as soon as we got engaged, we rarely went to his apartment anymore. When I got up the courage to suggest, 'Why don't we go to your place?' he said he was jet-lagged or he needed to get up early."

"How did you feel?" Dr. Schneider asked in typical therapist fashion.

6

"Humiliated and rejected, but I thought it would change once we were married."

"And what's happening now?" asked the good doctor.

"He's mostly working, traveling, or sleeping. I'm so frustrated. I don't know what to do."

Dr. Schneider sat forward in his brown leather desk chair, looked straight at me, and replied, "Look, if you wanted to get laid every night, you should have married a truck driver, not a nice Jewish boy. Jewish boys put their energy into their careers and building a life to take care of their families."

My face flushed, and I looked down at my hands. Shamed for my "whorish tendencies," I couldn't make eye contact. I left hastily and never went back.

And eighteen years later, there I was, sitting outside my white colonial house with the dark green shutters, preparing to sell it to finalize my divorce. I took a last drag of my cigarette and stood up. Time to pick up my kids. I got into my car and drove down the driveway, and as I passed the forsythia bush, I asked myself, *Am I, too, ready to bloom?*

OPA

July 1976

"I wonder if they have any nude beaches here?" I asked my best friend, Barbara. It was three months after the dumpster crunch, and we were sitting across from each other in a bustling seaside café on the island of Mykonos. I breathed in deeply, taking in the salty air.

"Great idea. Why don't you ask the waiter?"

"Okay," I said hesitantly. "I will . . . when he comes over."

I started to dive into the plate of moussaka in front of me, and Barbara held up her drink. "Here's to Greece," she said. "Five whole weeks without the school, our kids, or our husbands."

Barbara and I had been friends for thirteen years. We'd met as parent volunteers at a Montessori nursery school, then co-founded an innovative open education school where we'd shared an office for the past eight years. We were each other's "go-to" person, but we'd never been away on our own together.

"Oh, I'm so done with the husband part. I just need Myles

8

to sign the divorce papers." I poured a little more wine from the carafe. "I'm actually liking this Greek retsina. The pine taste is growing on me."

Barbara beamed as a tanned man with thick dark hair wearing a collarless white shirt strode by. She lowered her voice. "Suzy, look at these men with their gorgeous olive skin. All the aquiline noses and dark curly hair. It's like we're surrounded by Greek gods."

"Yeah, I couldn't help but notice, though, as we walked over here from the pension, we may have been looking at the men, but nobody seemed to be looking at us. I know we're forty, not twenty, but still . . ."

"Is that what you're here for, Suzy?"

"No, not really. I want to relax after winding up the school year, getting the kids off to their summer activities, prepping for the teacher training program in August. I'm just here to unwind and explore the Greek Islands with you."

Barbara nodded. "All we have to do now is find out if there's a nude beach. The waiter is about to come over. Are you ready to ask him?"

"No, you," I said sheepishly.

"Suzy, you're the one who came home from La Jolla two summers ago all aglow about experiencing a nude beach. You go away by yourself for the first time in your life to participate in a world-famous person-centered psych training program, and when you come back, all you talk about is the nude beach, the nude beach. This is not the time to be shy; the waiter is coming over—right now."

I looked up at the sleek, dark-eyed twenty-something waiter.

"Can I bring you ladies anything else?"

"The check would be great," I said. He was about to walk away when Barbara peered at me, her expression imploring me to speak up.

"Wait. Actually, we have a question." I hesitated and looked at Barbara for reinforcement. "We were, you know, just kind of wondering if maybe there are any beaches on Mykonos where you don't have to wear a bathing suit?"

Answering as casually as if I'd just asked for the dessert menu, he told us exactly where to go and how to get on the right boat. "And make sure you do not get off at the first stop; wait for the second," he said. Barbara and I smiled at one another as he left the table, lifting our now empty wine glasses.

———

The beach was perfect—deep blue water, crackling waves, pure white sand, and a crowd of casually naked people frolicking, swimming, and tanning. We sat on our towels, taking in the sights and the sound of the surf as we oiled ourselves up. Then we stretched out on our backs, closed our eyes, and surrendered. My hesitancy about asking the waiter seemed absurd. I was in heaven.

"Oh, that sun feels so delicious," Barbara said, practically humming. "When I open my legs to take it in, I could almost have an orgasm."

"Umm." I purred. "I can feel it penetrating all the way up. I can hardly lie still." Savoring the sensations, I finally asked, "Do you think you could really have an orgasm . . . without touching yourself?"

Barbara answered pretty quickly. "I think so."

"Hmm . . . Could I ask you another question?"

"Of course. Why would you even ask if you could ask?"

"I've never talked to anyone about this, man or woman—about what I like."

"I haven't either," Barbara admitted. "Though sometimes I make comments like, 'Oh, that feels so good.'"

"Yeah, positive reinforcement."

"And because lots of things feel so good."

"I know. But, well, here's my question. They make it sound like orgasm comes from inside, but I think mine really come from my clit. I've wondered if there's something wrong with me."

"I don't think so. It's the magic button."

"Whew. I'm glad to hear you say that. I guess what I don't understand is, with all the jokes about men getting to first base, second base, third base, they must know we like to be touched in all those places, but for them, it's all about scoring a home run. And sex scenes in movies don't have much foreplay either."

"True—lots of flirting, not much caressing. But there's a simple answer for that: All the movies we grew up on were made by men. Still are."

I lay there in the sun, thinking about how society shapes our views and how little I actually knew. Sex just wasn't talked about. Until I got married, I could hardly believe my parents even had sex. "Do you think it changes when you're married?"

"Maybe. There's a trade-off. There's less flirtation, but more giving each other pleasure."

"Hmmm. I guess I just don't know how to ask for what I want. It's so hard to talk about it." We were both quiet for a moment. And then I went on, grabbing the opportunity to keep the conversation going. "Okay, I've got another question. Did you masturbate when you were little?"

"I did, but always under the covers," she responded. "I don't remember when I started or how I got the message it was something to hide, but it was always guiltily under the covers. I also remember playing doctor when we were kids, but that was more about exploring the differences, not about pleasure."

"I only played with girls. Never anything sexual. Until high school, that is. Then I played for real with my boyfriend, all hands and mouths and rubbing against each other. I was always embarrassed about my panties getting damp. When he came back from the navy after college, we talked about how I remained technically a virgin even though I stayed over in his fraternity house. He said it was only because he didn't know any better. Honestly, though, I got more pleasure from all our petting when I was still a virgin."

We were quiet again for a few minutes, then I said, "Okay, another question. Did you ever masturbate in front of a man or touch yourself while you're having sex?"

"Unh-unh."

"Is that a no?"

"It's a no. Why? Have you?"

"I couldn't. What I did was grind my clit into him while we were having sex, so I got both things at once, which worked, thankfully. If I'd actually touched myself while we were lovemaking, I think Myles would have taken it personally, like I was telling him he wasn't doing a good job."

"That might have been the truth."

"But that would've hurt his feelings, and we'd have ended up having even less sex. Thank God this isn't about Myles anymore. I want to be free to enjoy my body. I want the courage to talk about what gives me pleasure."

We each got lost in our own thoughts and the delicious warmth of the sun on our bodies. I don't remember who said, "I have an idea. The sun-fucking is turning me on. When we get back to the pension, let's take turns being alone in the room."

"Great idea."

"A half hour?"

"I'm so turned on, fifteen minutes should be plenty."

———

Eventually, we left Mykonos to explore some other islands. On Skiathos, we met an older Greek American man whose long-haired teenage son skateboarded around town just like Barbara's sons. His son called him Papa, so we did too. Papa looked just like Aristotle Onassis. One evening, as Barbara and I were browsing the shops along the harbor, Papa came along, linked his arms in ours, and led us up a narrow winding street to a taverna in the old part of town, away from the tourist spots along the harbor. When he told us he lived on Sutton Place in Manhattan, we felt like we'd manifested our own rich Greek, just like Jackie Kennedy.

The bartender and a few men seated at the bar greeted Papa as we entered. This taverna didn't look like the usual bustling tourist cafés with their ubiquitous white stucco and bright blue tile. The room was lined with dark wood paneling and filled with dark furniture. Amber candles cast a warm glow from the few occupied tables, and a bouzouki player strummed softly in a corner. Papa shouted a greeting to him, and though it may have been my imagination, I would have sworn that the music got louder and faster. Papa ushered us to a table, then shouted something across the floor to the bartender. A waiter appeared with three shot glasses of ouzo and two small glasses of ice. As he poured our ouzo over the ice, it turned milky white. Papa raised his shot glass and shouted, "*Ya mas!*"

Barbara and I clinked our glasses with him and took a sip, while he downed his shot with one gulp. I smiled, savoring the licorice flavor that reminded me of my father's favorite candy, which he'd always kept in a covered dish next to his easy chair. Papa proceeded to call for one shot of ouzo after another. The bouzouki player egged him on. Suddenly, Papa jumped up, raised his arms, and started dancing. Barbara and I were mesmerized. The scene was right out of *Zorba the Greek*.

But that wasn't all. While he was dancing, Papa called out again to the waiter. We thought he was ordering another ouzo to fuel his dancing, but instead, the waiter brought a stack of plates. One by one, as he danced, Papa grabbed a plate, shouted "Opa!" and wildly flung it on the floor. When the stack was gone, he called for another stack, then another. Cheered on by the bouzouki and the patrons shouting, "Opa!" he joyfully smashed one plate after the next. With the crash of each plate, I felt exhilarated, just like I'd felt three months earlier as I heaved bag after bag of Myles's old mail into the garbage dumpster. With each crash, I felt the cocoon in which I'd lived my whole life shattering, freeing me to discover who I wanted to be—whatever that was going to be. *Opa!*

# SECOND ADOLESCENCE

November 1976

As I drove across the George Washington Bridge and down the West Side Highway into Manhattan, I gave myself a pep talk. *It's been four months since you returned from Greece. You're almost forty-one. You've got to start dating here, now, before it's too late.* I realized I was gripping the steering wheel tightly, so I took a deep breath, then leaned over and turned off the radio. *What do I want? To attract a guy. To have some fun. To be reassured that I am a desirable woman.* In the silence of the car, I let out a deep sigh and allowed myself to feel the empty, lonely place in my heart. I yearned for tenderness, appreciation, and companionship. It hit me that I hadn't experienced those things from a man. Ever.

Feeling needy was not comfortable. I turned the radio back on and headed to the Universalist church on Central Park West and Seventy-Fifth Street. I'd heard that three hundred people lined up outside the church every Friday night for the possibility of meeting someone of the opposite sex in a more humane setting than a singles bar. And, to avert the loneliness of the holiday season, a special event was held once a year on the Wednesday night before Thanksgiving. This pre-Thanksgiving gathering of hopeful singles was my destination.

It was the seventies—the decade after the assassinations of John Kennedy, Robert Kennedy, and Martin Luther King Jr., and the end of the first civil rights movement. The Beatles had visited, Woodstock had exploded onto the scene, and the culture had broken wide open with "sex, drugs and rock & roll." I had almost missed all the fun.

In the year and a half since we'd split, Myles had never taken all three of our daughters overnight at the same time. When he promised the girls an outing, he usually came late or didn't show up at all. My older girls, Wendy, sixteen, and Donna, fourteen, mostly shrugged him off and hung out with their high school friends, but our youngest, Sharrin, was only ten, and he consistently disappointed her. So, when he called to say he wanted to take all three girls to spend Thanksgiving weekend visiting his sister Bunny in Massachusetts, I told myself—*I MUST capitalize on the opportunity.*

I found a parking space, locked my car, buttoned up my coat, and walked three blocks to join the line of singles entering the church. *Would I have the courage to take off my coat when I got inside? What was I thinking going braless?* When I tucked my blue-and-rose print shirt into my jeans, I had been sure that the pattern covered my nipples, but still . . . going braless was a big step for a woman raised on panty girdles and structured bras.

Throughout my childhood and adolescence, my mother was the only mother I knew who had a career. She commuted with my father from Long Island into the city every day and then came home and took care of household, family, and social affairs. She didn't have time for tenderness. I never wanted to juggle career and family like her. I thought I would be a sweet, nurturing, stay-at-home mom, but somehow, I had backed myself into a career in education—and I'd found I loved it. After Myles and I split, it was even easier to integrate my life with my daughters and our life at the school. Until our house was sold, it was brimming on weekends with teenagers hanging out with my older daughters in our basement. The school community was like an extended family, protecting my girls and me from much of the isolation experienced by other single-mom families.

But there was still an empty space in my life. I hoped it wasn't too late.

The vast main hall of the church was filled with circles of gray folding chairs. I paid my five dollars and was given a number telling me which group to join. Group thirteen, my lucky number. *Stand up straight*, I told myself. *Look confident.*

As soon as I sat down, I spotted an attractive guy directly across from me in the circle. He had a great head of straight, silky brown hair, the kind you just want to run your fingers through—especially if your recent ex-husband was bald. I took in his neatly pressed jeans, his loafers, and his casual-chic blue-and-white checked shirt under a navy V-neck sweater—and wrote him off. *He's too young. He probably goes for the twenty-year-olds. Oh well.*

But after the group was over, he headed toward me and said, "I liked how you stopped that woman who was going on and on complaining about her ex. I couldn't come up with a tactful way to say, "Shut up," but you did it so nicely, like a pro."

I looked into his eyes and offered a smile. My mind was racing. *He's even better looking close-up. Such smooth skin.*

"I'm Charlie. Would you like to get a drink?" he asked.

"That'd be great."

He commandeered two clear plastic cups filled with white wine and led me to a wooden church pew that had been pushed against a side wall.

"I may have sounded like a pro, but I feel like a virgin," I admitted. "This is my first time at one of these things."

He nodded sympathetically. "I remember how weird I felt two years ago when I first started going out after my divorce. Good for you for taking this step. It's not easy."

Charlie was a social worker, and he knew how to ask the right questions to get me to open up. We didn't stop talking until they blinked the lights to empty the hall. As we went to get our coats, he invited me for a drink at a local watering hole. Ten minutes later, as we sat in a cozy, dimly lit West Side bistro, he asked, "If you could change one thing about your marriage, what would it be?"

I thought for a bit, then confessed, "Well, what really hurt was that he didn't want me sexually. His only passion was business. If the sex had been okay, maybe I could have accepted the rest."

The conversation flowed effortlessly. At some point, Charlie leaned in and asked, "Do you like oral sex?" A groan may have slipped out of my throat. I could only nod, but he must have read a hungry look on my face. We decided he would follow me home. At 2:00 a.m., with no traffic, it was only a twenty-minute drive from the Upper West Side to my house in Tenafly, New Jersey. We parked our cars near the back door. Butterflies filled my stomach. From my first venture out alone as a single woman, I was bringing home a great-looking, sweet guy, for what just might be great sex. I felt awkward, but Charlie gave me a reassuring hug, and we went straight upstairs.

Shortly after we snuggled under the covers, he worked his way down my body and positioned his head between my legs. I started off caressing his silky hair, but soon I surrendered to humming in delicious pleasure. After I shuddered and spasmed to climax, I sat right up and said, "Thank you," with indescribable gratitude. But he pushed me down gently, saying, "Oh, I'm not done yet."

The next morning, he greeted me with a smile and "Happy Thanksgiving." Then he suggested, "Let's get a guinea hen and make Thanksgiving together."

We started to solidify a plan when Barbara called to check on me. I told her my good fortune, and she invited Charlie and me to join her clan for dinner. It was my first Thanksgiving without my girls, and I was okay, even more than okay. I felt exhilarated, with an extra dollop of gratitude.

On our second date, at Charlie's studio apartment in Brooklyn Heights, he introduced me to Billy Joel's music. In particular, he played me a song with the line, "I don't know where I'm going, but I know what I'm leaving behind." I was touched that he had already grasped exactly where I was in my life, maybe more clearly than I did.

On alternate weekends, when he wasn't with his young daughter, he loved to hang out at my house and get stoned with my teenage girls and their friends from the Center, our high school. I was okay with them smoking pot on weekends, so long as they kept up with their schoolwork and didn't get high during the week. I was also happy to have them safe in the house, not out on the street or driving while stoned. Sitting around the kitchen table with my daughters and their closest friends gave Charlie a sense of belonging that he had not experienced during his own teenage years. When more teenagers arrived, they all went down to the basement with its big stone fireplace, beanbag chairs, and mirrored wall with a ballet barre left over from my girl's dancing days.

It was with Charlie that I began my dance with sex and drugs. Charlie had heard that quaaludes were great for sex, so I got us two of those little yellow hexagons, and Charlie planned a special stay-at-home evening in his apartment, a nice change for me from hanging out at my house. Charlie laid out the scenario. "We'll start with white wine, followed by the pills, then sex, then dinner," he explained. With the last sip of wine, we ceremoniously took the pills, stretched out on the bed, and went right to sleep. We awakened several hours later, both starving and disappointed; by the time we got around to sex, the drug had completely worn off.

Charlie also orchestrated my one and only psychedelic experience, and he did it with great care. We borrowed a tent from Wendy and went on a camping trip to Assateague Island in North Carolina, bringing with us two "sunshine" tablets for a "trip." Charlie had taken the drug once before and assured me it was a milder and more controllable trip than LSD.

Drugs were far less potent back in the seventies than they are today. We camped out for several nights, but for our "trip,"

Charlie insisted we shop around until he found what he considered the perfect motel room. "This is ideal," he said, with a smile and a little hug. "It has a comfortable bed and a balcony with views for as much outdoor experience as we might want."

When he unpacked a Scrabble set, I raised an eyebrow. "I thought we were going on a trip," I said.

"This," he assured me, "will focus your mind if you get uncomfortable and want to control the tripping." I remember two things vividly from the experience—a gorgeous nighttime sky ablaze with twinkling multicolored, not white, stars, and getting my very first ever seven-letter Scrabble word—APRICOT.

Charlie was certainly the right relationship at the right time. And he was the only man who ever bought me lingerie—sexy lace bikinis to replace the sturdy Pucci panties left over from my marriage that I was wearing the night we met. His attention gave me an intangible feeling of being appreciated I'd always longed for.

Until one day, after about six months, I walked into the kitchen and saw Charlie as just another teenager sitting around my big round white table. I felt it in my gut. I was done with my second adolescence. There was a world out there, and I wanted to join it as a free and independent adult.

# HELLO, WORLD

July 1977

I tried to act nonchalant as I wiggled out of my bikini bottoms and untied the strings of my top. After all, I was a proper New York Jewish girl, and we weren't raised to sunbathe naked. And yet here I was in Ibiza having my third nude beach experience. I was forty-one and on a trip to celebrate my divorce, which had finally been awarded.

As I stuffed my bikini into my beach bag and pulled out my suntan oil, I snuck a quick look at the nude form of my brand-new German lover stretched out next to me. Werner? Klaus? Fredrik? His name escapes me now, four decades later, but I do remember his smoldering dark eyes. He was the promise delivered of a new, sexually active life as a single woman.

Back then, in 1977, forty wasn't yet considered fabulous and divorce still carried a social stigma. However, the notion that women could have "zipless fucks" had garnered my attention when I read Erica Jong's *Fear of Flying*. I devoured that book as if it were a memoir, believing it was true, not a work of

23

fiction. Jong was a New York Jewish girl and an alumna of Barnard College, just like me. But she was six years younger than I, and what a difference that made. It was as if we were on opposite sides of a cultural divide. Her heroine had sexual adventures beyond my wildest dreams—but not beyond my yearnings.

Two weeks earlier, I had flown across the Atlantic by myself for the first time. I had no plan or program, just a desire to prove to myself that I could make it alone in the big world. My new German friend provided a guiding hand as I took my jump into this new realm as a single woman. In that hot July sun, with every inch of me exposed, I had never felt more alive. I was finding my path, fully aware in my natural state that I was living the international adventure I had barely even dreamed of only a few months before.

Getting to him—and that nude beach—hadn't been easy. I stretched out in the sun and reviewed the previous two weeks. On the flight to Spain, as I sipped my vodka tonic and stared out at the endless blue sky, I told myself, *Suzy, dear girl . . . You've got the world by the tail. You can do this.* Then I realized, though I had no fear of flying, I was also scared to death. I took a breath and asked myself, *Can I go out in the world, away from family, friends, the school—all my known tethers? Can I do it and do it well?* I ordered another vodka tonic.

Since I didn't speak any Spanish, I was pleased with how well I handled changing planes in Madrid and finding the right bus from the Málaga airport to Marbella. When I boarded the bus, I showed the driver the address of the free condo in Marbella that Barbara's friend had offered me. I sat in the front row anxiously, hoping the bus driver would alert me when we arrived. After a fifty-minute ride along a two-lane coastal road with mountains on one side and occasional peeks of the sea on the other, he stopped the bus, pointed to me, and then pointed across the street. It felt like he was dropping me off in the middle of nowhere. When the bus pulled out, there was not a soul around. I crossed the empty road to a long, dense strip of apartment buildings stretching as far as my eye could see.

While the condo turned out to be on a gorgeous beach, it was not walking distance to any stores, restaurants, or bars for the evenings. It would have been fine for a couple, but it was too isolated for my newly single self.

I studied my guidebook and picked out a destination in town: La Tricycletta, "an amiable hangout for expats." I took a shower, checked my guidebook again, then slipped into my white slacks and new black top and headed back out to the road to wait for the next bus into town. My condo turned out to be only fifteen minutes from the center of Marbella. Within a five-minute walk, I spotted the big tricycle sign. I was so relieved. No Spanish needed for that! The hosts, a friendly, attractive English couple, invited me to have a drink, then explained the crowd wouldn't begin to arrive until 11:00 p.m. I was hungry, and they didn't serve food, so I left, promising to return.

The next challenge, picking a restaurant, was immediately upon me. It was hard to choose an eatery from the street, especially when I didn't know the language, so I followed a family with children into a restaurant. It was filled with big round communal tables covered in white tablecloths. I was seated with the family and two other strangers. Nobody at our table spoke English, so conversation was a challenge. So was ordering. I played charades, silently signaling the waiter I would have the same as the nine-year-old girl. They brought us each a whole fish. The girl picked up her knife and fork and perfectly deboned hers. I wanted to hand her mine. I'd never learned to debone a fish. The only fish my mother served was boneless filet of flounder, which I hated. I didn't do much better by my children; I only broiled swordfish steaks, with no bones.

A while later, I returned to Tricycletta, happy to be back at a familiar place. As I walked through the door, the host called out, "Hi, Suzy, come meet the crowd." I liked being treated like a member of the family. A willowy blonde in a sexy red dress picked up her purse and patted a barstool. "Sit here, sweetie. I'm Maggie," she said. "What ya drinking?"

I ordered chardonnay and told Maggie I was a New Yorker celebrating my divorce.

"We're going dancing later," she said. "You've got to come. The disco gets hot around two a.m."

"I'd love to," I responded, not mentioning jet lag or that I didn't know how to dance without holding on to a partner.

This convivial group of Brits and Aussies owned or managed shops, bars, and restaurants in Marbella. They adopted me, and life fell into a rhythm. Sunning at the beach and catching up on lost sleep, socializing with "my crowd" at Tricycletta, then off to the discotheque at two in the morning for dancing, drinking, strobe lights, and ABBA. Each night, the throbbing beat pulled me straight past the noisy bar and right onto the packed dance floor. I slithered my way into the middle of the crowd, feeling safely invisible in the smoke-filled haze. Then I raised my arms, rolled my hips, and surrendered to becoming a "Dancing Queen." Feigning nonchalance, I watched the gyrating moves of other dancers and tried to copy whatever looked good. It didn't matter with whom I was dancing; I was in the scene.

A few days in, I hooked up with an attractive guy from California. To a newly minted New York divorcée, a Californian was as exotic as a European. At lunch one day with two other couples at a restaurant on the beach, we caught the eye of Xaviera Hollander, the infamous former $1,000-a-night call girl and successful New York City madam, whose memoir, *The Happy Hooker,* had sold millions of copies worldwide several years earlier. Xaviera had been jailed in New York and then deported back to Holland, but a subsequent Hollywood movie had kept her story very much alive. With her bleached blond hair and flamboyant clothes, she was definitely still playing the part as she made herself the center of attention. Without leaving her seat, she looked over at the six of us at my table and asked, "Who's with whom?" After ascertaining that my guy was single, she flirted with him in earnest. When we stood up to leave, she wiggled her finger at him, but he took my hand, and we ambled over to her table together. She invited the two of us for cocktails at the home of a friend. I was intrigued to go. In fact, I couldn't wait to see what a night out with the Happy Hooker might look like.

Our white haired host played classical music for us on his white piano in his elegant all-white apartment, while Xaviera dropped her public persona entirely and seamlessly turned the pages of the music for him. They clearly were attuned to each other. I wondered what their relationship was—lover, friend, sugar daddy? They invited us to join them for dinner on the quiet terrace of a nearby restaurant overlooking the sea. Conversation flowed easily from culture to politics to travel. But then, as we were sipping our after-dinner coffee, a group of chic young European men arrived at our table and whisked Xaviera away, leaving us with her charming male companion.

I felt sorry for him. He was a handsome, cultured, dignified older man. I wondered how he felt about being dumped like that. But he continued talking, not the least bit nonplussed by her abrupt departure. I wondered: *Who is using whom? Or do they both like their relationship just the way it is?* I was turned off by the way she donned what looked to me like her "life as a performance" persona. I thought I valued authenticity, but was I just playing "the gay young divorcée" myself?

Loving the beach as I do, I "tried on" the expat beach town life, but, after two weeks, I decided I'd had enough. It was a little too alcoholic for me. *I don't want another drink to rev me up,* I thought, *and I can't walk into that disco one more time.* I was excited to realize—I didn't have to stay. For the first time in my life, I could do whatever I wanted.

I had another week until I had to return to work, though, and I certainly wasn't going to return home early. Instead, I bought a ticket to the island of Ibiza. It had been my second-choice destination after Marbella. I wondered if it would be like the fabulous chic isle of Capri on my honeymoon, or like the simple, charming Greek Islands I'd explored last summer with Barbara.

My new Marbella "friends" tried to discourage me from

moving on. They warned, "You can't go to Ibiza in the summer without booking a room in advance." But I was in Spain to prove to myself I could travel on my own, so off I went.

I landed in Ibiza, happy to have escaped from the beat of the Marbella disco and ready for a new adventure on this famous little island. But first, I had to get back to basics: *Find a hotel.* In the middle of the airport lobby, I spotted a tourist kiosk. "Have you a room in a beachfront hotel?" I asked with some trepidation.

"Oh, yes," she replied, pulling out a card. "I have one right here at La Paloma. You are lucky, the bus to the hotel will be leaving shortly." I was relieved. *See, I can go without a reservation*, I said smugly to my Marbella chorus.

Night had fallen by the time the bus pulled up to a sleek, modern hotel. *Wow*, I thought, *I've scored.* I entered the granite lobby, got my room key, and was directed to go right to dinner. The dining room was noisy, and within seconds it was clear everyone seemed to know each other. *Oops.* They were all speaking German. I had found a room at the beach, but it was in a German tour group hotel—all families with children and out in the middle of nowhere.

I studied my guidebook and saw there were lots of hotels in Ibiza Town, with boats from the harbor to nearby beaches. I checked out the next morning and took a local bus for a long ride into town. I got off the bus, lugging my heavy suitcase, and faced a line of hotels on the main drag. I thought, *Ugh, no charm*, but at least there were lots of places to stay.

First hotel, "no rooms." Second hotel, "no rooms." It was the same at my next stop and the next and the next. I kept working my way down the strip. Midway, I stopped asking for an ocean-view room. I just wanted a room. Soon, I began cursing my suitcase.

*Was every hotel really fully booked? Was I picking up an attitude from the front desk clerks? Did they not like Americans?* I kept walking. It was getting late; I'd been walking the street for hours. Then a thunderbolt struck: *Oh my God, they must think I'm a streetwalker! After all, what proper woman shows up alone to Ibiza without a reservation or a husband?*

My shoulders tensed. My breathing became shallow. I started to feel desperate but tried not to succumb to panic. I was beginning to feel like eight-year-old me, lost at Columbus Circle in New York City. That time I cried until some nice lady stopped, said, "Little girl, can I help you?" and led me to a pay phone to call my mommy. Mommy couldn't rescue me now. I was forty-one years old, and I was in Ibiza. *Oh, why did I push my luck?* I asked myself. *I shouldn't have left Marbella. What should I do? What should I do?*

And then, just off the main street, I spotted a real estate office that was still open, and I charged right over. They had a furnished studio apartment near the harbor available to rent by the week. Sight unseen, I paid and took the key. However dirty or grungy, it was a solution.

The studio turned out to be delightfully clean and white, with a little view of the harbor. First order of business, I headed straight for the bathroom, where I promptly discovered there was no toilet paper. And then, I was hit by a second bolt of lightning. *This is my first apartment. Just for me. I will have to buy toilet paper just for me, not for family. Toilet paper just for me for the first time in my life.* In the years to come, looking back, I would realize this sounded silly, but at the time, it was monumental. I'd never lived alone before. I went down to the street and found a bodega. I wanted to exclaim to the clerk, "My first toilet paper just for me!" but my lack of Spanish locked my joy inside. I felt myself connecting to the generation after mine, to all those women who lived in their first apartments and bought toilet paper for themselves before they married and had families.

The next morning, I headed down to the harbor to catch whatever boat was leaving for a beach. On the big outboard motorboat with about twenty people, I sat in silence. Lots of languages, but no one spoke English. I wished I was multilingual. I was beginning to miss my Marbella friends.

I followed the crowd off the boat and noticed that the Spanish speakers settled into beach chairs, but the Scandinavians and Germans moved on. I followed them, hoping for something a little less formal—no beach chairs and lawns. We walked around the bluff and down a path and voilá—a topless beach! There hadn't been any nudity in Marbella, at least not where I was staying or with the expat crowd that took me in. I stretched out my towel and oiled up; I was a happy camper with fellow European sun worshippers. At the end of the day, as I joined the trek back to the boats, a sexy, dark-eyed German said something to me. With a helpless shrug, I told him I only spoke English. When he replied in English, I lit up. We talked all the way back on the boat, made a date for dinner, and after dinner, he spent the night.

I was beaming the next morning as we chatted away on the boat on which I'd felt so isolated the day before. When we arrived at the beach, he led me past the Spaniards in their bathing suits and beach chairs, and one level below, past the topless Scandinavians where I had perched the day before. Leading me further on, he took my beach bag and held my hand to help me climb down a somewhat treacherous bluff to this perfect little cove with a beautiful beach. I looked around. Everyone was nude. I was thrilled to have manifested not only a beautiful nude beach but a sexy German lover with whom to share it.

While I baked in the sun, lost in a reverie about my whole Spanish adventure, I was startled when my new friend suddenly sat up and said, "I'll be right back." It was like being awakened from a delicious sleep. I wasn't quite ready. But a little while later he returned, saying "I hope you're hungry." He was holding fresh fish, grilled by an enterprising local right there on the beach. I sat up to share this delicious treat. As I looked around, I realized everyone was German. They had all arrived, as we did, by climbing down the bluff.

I was savoring the ambience and loving that I was the only American when suddenly a speedboat raced in with a buxom, nude German mama proudly standing on the prow, her blond hair streaming in the wind. Her husband steered right up onto the beach, and their three beautiful nude children jumped out. I was so happy to be part of this scene. I'd made it. I'd faced some challenges, bought my toilet paper, and now I felt like that German mama.

*Hello, world*, I thought. *Here I am!*

# PLAYMATE

Spring 1978

"Tonight's the night. We're going to Plato's Retreat," my boyfriend, Syd, announced when I arrived at his apartment one Friday night.

"Oh, no," I said, "I can't go to Plato's tonight."

"Why not?"

"Look how I'm dressed—all preppy." I was wearing my favorite school director garb of gray flannel pants and gray cashmere turtleneck sweater under a dark green double-breasted Anne Klein blazer.

Syd was my second post-Myles boyfriend, after Charlie. When I'd returned from the nude beach in Spain nine months earlier, Syd had introduced me to the nude beach in Kismet, a town on Fire Island for over-forty singles, and we'd spent the rest of the summer weekends out there together. He was the same body type as Myles, my father, and the majority of Jewish men of my generation and earlier: no more than five foot eight or nine, receding hairline, tending toward middle-age paunchiness in the midsection. Syd owned a successful wholesale business, was legally separated from his wife, and was very attentive to his young daughter and son. When he took me and my daughters out to celebrate my forty-second birthday in January, the thought had crossed my mind that he might be a potential second husband—a nice, bright, balding Jewish man, but this time, one who liked sex.

On this night, he pulled back from his welcoming hug and laughed. "It doesn't matter what you're wearing. Clothes-off is a condition of being there."

I gulped. "You're right, of course. Okay, but I'll need some help to get up the courage to walk through the door."

Syd was into sexual adventuring, not drugs, and really only shared a joint, pill, or sniff with me to help me overcome my inhibitions to play.

"Don't worry. We're well supplied. What do you want now? Pot, coke, or a quaalude? I'll take the rest with us."

"Can we do drugs openly there?"

"I don't know, but we'll find out. It sounds like quite a scene. I'll be fun."

We'd read about Plato's Retreat: a nude sex club in the basement of a hotel on the Upper West Side. The article Syd showed me said Plato's had swimming pools, a disco, a café, lounges, and a large pillow room with a mirrored ceiling.

"Yes, it would be fun to see, but only to see. I don't want any stranger touching me."

"I agree. But what about us?" he asked with a twinkle in his eye and a sly grin. "It might be fun to play with each other."

"Uh-huh." I nodded and grinned back. "As long as we agree to stick together and no sex with anyone else."

In the car on the way uptown, the quaalude I'd taken made me feel relaxed and alert at the same time. I liked it. The Ansonia Hotel didn't have a parking garage, but we found one nearby. As we walked toward the hotel, I started to get nervous, so we took a toke or two of a joint in a dark doorway before entering the lobby. The hotel was past its prime, no big bouquet of flowers, not even potted palms to distract from the chipped paint and tarnished brass. The desk clerk took one look at us, pointed to the elevator, and said, "The basement."

Syd paid the membership fee for us as a couple. Single men were not allowed, but single women were. The man collecting the money at the door handed each of us a white towel and informed us, "The bar and buffet and use of all the facilities are included in the membership fee. To get to the locker room, make a left turn just before the bar."

"Ah," I said to Syd. "That solves the question of how you carry cash or a credit card for food and drink if you don't have a pocket."

It was probably only a one-minute walk from the entrance to the locker room, but—ever my mother's daughter— I immediately focused in on the fashion, in this case, how the women were wearing their skimpy white towels. There seemed to be three choices: wrapped around and tucked in near the armpit to cover the breasts down to the top of the thighs like I tucked my larger towel at home; wrapped and tucked around the waist, leaving the breasts bare; or tossed around the neck to casually fall over the nipples. I opted for the second choice, covering up my less-than-flat tummy. Syd tried wrapping his towel around his waist too, but the beginnings of a potbelly got in the way and the towel fell right off. He nonchalantly picked it up and tossed it over his shoulder.

I thought Syd was the adventurous leader in our play, but years later, he told me he wouldn't have had the courage without my hand to hold as we stretched the boundaries during our experiences together.

We passed a small swimming pool, and Syd suggested, "Let's go in. We can have it all to ourselves."

We enjoyed a lap or two of nude swimming, then started fooling around with each other, first in the pool, then stretched out on the edge. All of a sudden, Syd stopped caressing me. I sat up on my elbow and asked, "What's up? Why did you stop?"

Syd whispered, "Over there. See the bleachers. People are sitting there watching us."

Without hesitation, I replied, "I'm so glad I'm here and we're the ones having the fun, not there, just sitting in the dark watching." I leaned in and kissed him, surprised to realize that I was turned on by the discovery that people were watching. I didn't know I had an exhibitionist in me.

I was delighted to be in the parade, rather than watching it pass me by. And I wondered, *Where will it take me?*

# LEAVING HOME

April 1979

I'd made a big decision, an enormous decision. It had hit me out of the blue, and I wanted to tell Barbara immediately. But she was off on a camping trip with the middle-school teachers and kids, so I had to wait twenty-four hours until she returned. She called me late on Sunday afternoon, and I could barely pay attention as she told me all about the camping trip.

Finally, I burst in. "Barbara, I cannot wait any longer. There's something important I have to tell you."

"What? Are you okay? What's the matter?"

"I've decided to leave the school."

"What? Leave the school? Suzy, you can't. That's crazy. This is our thing."

"I know," I said.

"And we created it together. I can remember the night you quit Montessori like it was yesterday, how you threw a tantrum because the board wouldn't let you bring non-Montessori materials into the school. Remember?"

"Of course. Not my finest moment. I was so frustrated, I

quit and walked out. And then I called you the next morning, crying hysterically because I'd ended a career I hadn't even known I'd wanted."

The memories came back clearly. After I calmed down, I'd called Nancy Rambusch, who had written the wonderful book *Learning How to Learn*, which had started the Montessori movement in America. It wasn't the first time I'd called Nancy. The first fateful phone call to her was in late 1963, when I'd asked her to run a Montessori teacher training program, and she said, "If you run it, I'll teach in it." We'd done just that, and the experience had become my private tutorial, one that turned out to be better than a graduate degree in education.

It had also led to the start of Barbara and I working together. When I'd enrolled Barbara's almost four-year-old daughter in the Montessori school in the spring of 1964, I'd also "enrolled" Barbara to take over some of the school administration because I was so busy with the teacher training program.

So, the call I made four years later, after my tantrum resignation and crying hysterically with Barbara, was the second fateful phone call I'd made to Nancy. When I told her about the board's refusal to allow plastic post-Montessori learning materials, Nancy said without a beat, "Suzy, start your own school." Barbara also resigned from the Montessori school, Nancy got us corporate backing, and we started the Children's Center.

"From the start, it's been an incredible experience," Barbara said. "And the school is a wonderful place. You can't leave."

"It's time, Barbara. It's been eleven years since we started, six since we hired Mike and opened the high school. And the truth is, you and Mike can manage without me. It's time for me to move on."

"But you can't go without me," Barbara said. "I'm not even divorced yet. I haven't thought beyond that."

"I get it. I never thought beyond getting divorced either." Our salaries at the school and our whole "embededness" in the school community had made it easier for Barbara and me to split from our husbands and our whole New York Jewish upbringing, because we still had the security of each other and the school.

"So, what changed? This is crazy!"

"What changed is that over the weekend I did the school budget for next year, and I realized that with this recession, the school will no longer be able to afford you and Mike and me. And I decided I want to be the one to go. You and Mike and the teachers can manage without me."

"No, that doesn't make sense. Let's you and I go over the budget together tomorrow. We'll figure it out. It can't be that different."

"What's different is I cut back on enrollment projections for next year. The handwriting is on the wall. With this recession, the pendulum has swung back from liberal to conservative. More parents are deciding private school is a luxury they can't afford. Even lower-school parents are asking, 'How can I be sure my child will get into a good college and get a good job when they grow up?' Trusting their children to be self-directing has suddenly become more of a luxury than a core belief. With two administrators, not

39

three, the school will be fine, even if somewhat fewer students are enrolled."

"But Suzy, we've been sharing this vision and our office and our lives for so long, I can't imagine being there without you. What will you do?"

"Now that I'm divorced, I want to get out of Tenafly and move into the city. I'll get a job as a human resource director with a corporation, doing what I do here but making big bucks. When Donna graduates in June, I'll 'graduate' too."

"Wow, I have to admit, that sounds good. I wish I could leave with you, but Gary has one more year at the Center, and then Peter will just be starting high school. Wait, what are you going to do about Sharrin? She's got another year of middle school too."

"I just talked to her."

"You did? What'd she say?"

"Well, as you can imagine, she's shocked. She said, 'Mom, you've been the school director my whole life.'"

Barbara chimed in, "It's all she's ever known."

"But not to worry," I went on. "She told me she didn't want to move to the city with me. She said, and I quote, 'I'd rather go to boarding school next year while you get your act together.'"

"Wow, that's pretty savvy of her. She told you just what you wanted to hear."

"That's not all. Then she looked me right in the eyes and asked, 'Mom, who are you if you're not the school director?'"

Barbara and I were both silent on the phone for a moment. Then I spoke. "Remember that song that Charlie played for me when I first met him, *'I don't know where I'm going, but I know what I'm leaving behind.* "Well, at least I know I'm going back to the city."

I *was* stripping off daily motherhood, home, school, and suburbia, totally unmindful of how it might feel to stand naked alone on the streets of New York.

# CRACKING THE SHELL

## Fall 1979

*Stop! I want off!* I startled and woke up on a friend's couch in Manhattan. In my dream, though, I was a white rat in a cage, endlessly running on a spinning wheel. *Stop the world, I want to get off* played over and over in my head. I released a huge sigh as I realized that, at age forty-three, I'd been running and juggling for years. I'd just quit the school, taken the summer off, sold the small post-divorce house, and moved to the city, but I wasn't ready to jump into a new corporate career. Instead of feeling excited and energized, I felt totally burnt out. *Am I turning out like my mother after all—tense and over-stretched? She had ulcers; I've got crippling back spasms. I need to stop and catch up with myself.*

As I lay there on my friend's couch, my mind jumped back four years to a monthlong summer workshop I'd taken at the Gestalt Institute in Amherst, Massachusetts, in 1975. An introductory experience in bioenergetics had intrigued me. I remembered lying on the floor among fifty people and being ordered to close my eyes and kick my legs. "Harder,

harder," the instructor was shouting. "Pound your arms and scream, 'NO, NO, NO!' Louder! Louder! Keep yelling!"

The room filled with the sound of "NO, NO, NO!"

I certainly would not have been able to scream on my own. But, empowered by the group, and with my arms and legs flailing, I joined in. "NO, NO, NO!" Eventually, from someplace deep inside, I connected to the rage I had locked away long ago. I didn't understand what it was all about, but I felt something, an energetic swell—and the surge was powerful. I made a mental note: *If I ever go into therapy, bioenergetics is the way I should go. Engaging my body might help me crack through my strong emotional defenses.*

And now, four years later, the time had come. I got off my friend's couch and made a phone call that would change my life. Instead of mobilizing myself to start a new career as I had expected when I left the Center and suburbia, I walked straight across Central Park to the Institute for the New Age on Seventy-Eighth Street, just off Madison Avenue. I had heard about the Institute from Barbara; her childhood friend was in training as a therapist there. Barbara had started in therapy too. Little did I know how profoundly I would be changed by this leap into the unknown recesses of my psyche.

I met Judith Schmidt, the therapist to whom I was assigned, in her office on the second floor of the Institute. Wasting no time, I plopped into a chair and the words spilled out. "In June I retired from a great career in education and thought I'd get an apartment and start a new career in the corporate world after the summer. But I just can't right now. I feel dead inside. I don't know who I am. I need to find my inner self."

Judith nodded and opened her book. "I can see you Tuesdays at two."

"No, not once or twice a week," I explained. "I'm not going to be working or having any family or household demands for the first time in my adult life. I'm staying at a friend's until my parents leave for Florida for the winter. They've agreed to let me stay in their apartment while they are gone. With no rent and some money from the sale of my house, I don't have to get a job right away. I want to make a full-time job of this . . . and I am in a hurry."

"Why are you in such a hurry?"

I straightened up in my chair and raised my eyebrows. I thought it was obvious. "I'm in a hurry because I'm forty-three years old, and I have three daughters. I want to create a new life, but I'm paralyzed. I have to find myself. I told you, I feel dead inside."

Judith agreed to see me three times a week. I also joined a weekly therapy group and other activities at the Institute. It wasn't easy to crack through the strong defenses that had helped me function successfully for so long. The severe muscle spasms in my lower back that had plagued me during the last few years of my marriage got even more debilitating.

"Yell! Stamp your feet! Swing the padded bataka bat, or thwack that old tennis racket against the couch!" Judith directed me to try them all. Climbing the stairs to her office was tortuous when my lower back was in spasm; by the time I reached the top, I was sometimes near tears from the pain. "Bend over this and breathe," she directed, pointing to the padded wooden stand I came to call "the rack." It hurt so much, but it did open me up.

From my previous taste of bioenergetics in Amherst, I knew there was childhood pain and anger somewhere deep inside me, but I wasn't able to find it for months. I felt I had terrific parents who, in their late seventies and early eighties, were still there for me. When I'd asked, they'd agreed to let me live in their Manhattan apartment when they left for the winter in Florida so I could afford to not work for a while and go on an inner journey. I'd been such a high performer for so long, my mother was scared I was having a nervous breakdown. My parents had even offered to pay for my therapy. It was hard to allow myself negative feelings toward them.

Judith asked, "What is your earliest childhood memory?"

I thought for a while and finally said, "I guess it was when I got diarrhea in the swimming hole at sleepaway camp when I was three."

"Three!" she exclaimed. "You went to sleepaway camp when you were three?"

Without any emotion, I explained, "There was a polio epidemic in the city. My mother said my big brother would look after me." I shrugged. "Of course, he didn't. He ignored me at camp just like he did at home."

Judith had me stand up, bend my knees a little, and shake until the energy began moving through my body. Then she handed me the bataka and told me to beat it against the couch while she asked me, "What do you want to tell your mother? Tell her. Tell her," over and over again. "Keep beating. Tell her. Bend your knees. Keep beating. Tell her."

Eventually, I blurted out, "I don't believe you sent us away because of the polio epidemic. Mal was old enough for camp, but I was only three! I think you just didn't want me underfoot while you were moving."

Judith had me continue to beat with the bataka until the dam burst and my sobs began. Once they started, I thought they would never stop. But she knew better.

There were sessions when I'd still be crying, and Judith would tell me, "Our time is up for today. I'm going to get myself a cup of tea. Let yourself out when you're ready. I'll see you next time." I learned a profound lesson from her behavior. I learned that it was safe to go to the dark, vulnerable places. She trusted I would come back. Each time I fell apart, I eventually got myself back together and left.

"What was it like in your house when you were growing up?" Judith once asked. I paused, shrugged, stayed silent. I shifted around on the gray tweed couch, looked over at Judith in her padded wooden rocker, then stared blankly at the window.

"What comes up first?"

"Well, it was lonely. My parents left every morning before I woke up and came home on the 6:13 Long Island Railroad train from the city. If I tried my brother's door to see if he was reading in his room, he threatened, 'Close that door and leave me alone or I'll hit you.' If he did swat me and I tattled, my mom always said, 'You shouldn't have bothered him.' Mal was six years older and didn't want anything to do with me until I was a teenager, so I was like a lonely only child. All my friends had younger siblings . . . and mothers at home. My mother was the only mother who worked."

"How did you feel about that?" Judith asked.

"Well, I knew she was doing something important, not

playing mahjong or canasta like some of my friend's moms. But she had so much to do with her work, and my father, and us, and the house, and her friends, and the relatives, and entertaining, and, and, and. She was such a perfectionist; she was always so tense. She and my father fought all the time."

"What about?"

"The business. That summer they sent me to sleepaway camp when I was three, they moved out to Rockville Centre from the city, but then my dad decided to start an advertising business, and he asked my mom to come help him. She did all the financial things, and he was the creative marketing man. The agency was very successful, but he never acknowledged how important she was in managing it all. Today she'd be called both the chief financial officer and the human resource director, but in those days, she was happier to keep a low profile because being a career woman was not what women did. A trade magazine called my dad 'The Madison Avenue Maverick.' It was her job to rein him in. So, they came home fighting every night, and they continued at the dinner table."

"Close your eyes and take a few breaths, then go back to your childhood. You hear your parents at the door. Tell me what's happening and how you feel."

"I'm sitting on the landing with my feet on the wooden step into the kitchen, talking to Parthenia, our housekeeper. Night after night, I sat there waiting for my parents. She let me sit there and talk while she made dinner but never invited me in to help. She, like my mother, didn't want me underfoot.

"I hear my parents walking up the front steps, so I jump up to greet them. My mother doesn't like me crowding them at the front door, so I wait impatiently for them to walk through the foyer. I get 'Hi, Suzy' from both of them, but Daddy's comes with a grin on his face and wide-open arms. Mom gives me a pat on the head, but she proceeds right past me to hang up her coat, organizing and ordering like she's still in the office. She says, 'I'm going to wash my hands for dinner. Have you washed yours?' I nod yes, and she continues, 'I'll check on dinner with Parthenia. You go upstairs. Get your brother. I'm not allowed to call upstairs to him. That's not ladylike.'

"Then we take our seats on the green covered chairs at the shiny wood table on our green carpeted floor in our green painted dining room, always in the same seats. As Parthenia brings in the golden chicken, I try, 'You'll never guess what—' but Mom interrupts to tell me to pass the mashed potatoes, then the string beans, and my moment is lost. Mal and I mutely watch the verbal ping-pong match."

"What's that sound like?" Judith asked.

"Okay. I remember this one fight like it happened yesterday." I sat up straight, my hands grasping Judith's couch cushion tightly, on full alert, bracing for the fight:

"My mother says to my dad, 'Emil, I couldn't ask you on the train or the bus with others around, but I want to hear what happened at your UJA luncheon today.'"

I explained to Judith, proudly, "My dad was the head of the advertising division of the United Jewish Appeal."

Judith suggested I close my eyes and asked, "What does your father say about the luncheon?"

"He says, 'It was great. We raised thirty thousand dollars.'"

"And my mother replies in that stern voice that means,

*You're in trouble!* 'Emil, I hope you didn't pledge as much as last year!'

"He just keeps munching on his chicken leg, and without looking up, he says, 'Actually, the need is more than twice as great this year with all the war refugees, so I doubled my pledge.'

"'Doubled it?' she says. 'And just where do you think we'll get the money?'

"My dad tells her she'll come up with it, that it's important. That they have no choice. That the situation is desperate.

"Mom is really angry now. She pushes away her plate, saying, 'Emil, we just don't have it. I'm still paying off last year's pledges. You cannot do this. You must stop!'

"Putting down his chicken leg, he looks her right in the eye. 'Terrible things are happening in Europe,' he says. 'We must help. I made the pitch and set the example today, and it worked. I got everyone to contribute more.'

"She starts to speak, but he interrupts. Turning to me, he says, 'If you're done, come give me a cuddle.' Then he gets up from the table and heads for his easy chair next to the fireplace in the living room."

"So, what do you do?" asked Judith.

"Oh, I hop off my chair and follow. Cuddles with Daddy are as sweet as dessert. It's my favorite thing. I know their argument isn't over. There will be raised voices later from their bedroom. And then maybe, after that, the icy atmosphere when my father is in the doghouse. She will punish him by not speaking to him directly for days, sometimes weeks. At the dinner table she'll say sternly. 'Tell your father . . . this,' or 'Ask your father . . . that.'"

49

I open my eyes. I don't want to feel that frigid air of my mother's anger. I tell Judith, "We were all the victims of her silent treatment. I hated when it was my turn. My mother was proud of her disciplining method. She thought it was 'lady-like.' Years later I realized she was a victim herself. She prided herself on not 'screaming like a fishwife'—that was her expression—but she swallowed so much rage, she ended up with stomach ulcers."

Judith has me stand up, take the bataka, bend my knees, and start thwacking the couch, thwacking and thwacking until the rage comes.

"Talk to me, Mommy. Stop being so mean. I hate this silence. I hate it. I hate it. I hate you."

One day, well into my second year with Judith, I recounted a terrifying dream I'd had the night before. Judith directed me to close my eyes and dive deeply into it.

"I am barely hanging on to the edge of a precipice. There is nothing to grab on to. I can't move my hands. I am losing my grip. I am down to the last knuckles. Below is the abyss."

"Look up," said Judith. "What can you see?"

Eventually I said, "I can see light."

"What can you do?"

"I don't know."

"At a time like that, I would pray," she said.

And so, I did.

I was not spiritual at all when I started in therapy. But what a gift that advice was. She reminded me that there was a greater force and I could connect to it. I consider that a peak moment in my therapy—actually, in my life.

Raised by my mother's mantra, "Stand on your own two

feet," and my father's dictum, "Plan your work and work your plan," I became a strong, independent person. It wasn't until therapy with Judith in my forties that I learned to acknowledge my shadow side—the hidden part of me that just wanted to be taken care of. I call that three-year period my "dark night of the soul" because after being so busy and so productive for so long, I was now lost in the outer world as I took the time to find and listen to my inner being.

The first two years I was back in the city, Barbara was still working at the Center and living in New Jersey. Although we talked on the phone all the time, it wasn't like the contact we had enjoyed for years while sharing the close quarters of our office. I tried to do some social things like playing tennis, but my heart wasn't in it, and I wasn't connecting to myself or to others. Some of my "sex, drugs and rock & roll" behavior wasn't just exploring the counterculture; it was numbing out and running away from my lonely, disconnected self. Often, on my way home from the Institute, in the bleak early dark of a New York winter, I stopped at Häagen-Dazs for a pint of solace for my dinner. Or was it a quart?

One clear night, I walked out onto my parents' terrace high above the East River. As I gazed across Manhattan, I saw all of those millions of lights, in all of those thousands of apartments where people seemed to be living as an interconnected web. But I felt so alone, on the outside looking in. It was the loneliest night of my life. Even now, when I hear the word "loneliness," I think of my disconnection on that terrace that night.

Now, forty years on the other side of therapy, I see clearly that all the pent-up emotions I released in those three years of inner work left me cleaner, clearer, and freer to be in the here and now. I no longer reacted to life so much through the filter of my past. In the years to come, I would see over and over again how people can be so victimized by their childhood story that they can neither embrace their present experience nor walk into the future unencumbered by their past.

This inner work represented a turning point to a new sense of self and spiritual awakening. And from that emerged a new life, one that would evolve over and over, in ways I could never have predicted.

# STARTING OVER

I took off my fur-lined gloves, then my gray furry earmuffs, unwrapped my gray wool scarf, and unzipped my purple down coat. I plopped down onto a chair and started rubbing my hands together, trying to get the bitter February chill out of my fingertips. My fingers and toes have never liked the cold. Even when my girls were young, I gratefully watched from indoors as they and our whole neighborhood enjoyed sleigh riding down our front hill. Now, at forty-six, it was even harder to get the circulation going.

As soon as everyone in my therapy group was seated, I announced, "I'd like to go first. I have something important to share." No one objected, so I proceeded. "I've decided to move to California. I'm going to leave for San Diego on July first."

The two therapists stayed silent, while one after another of the group members sputtered with incredulity. "Where did that come from?" "What's going on?" "What are you running away from?" "You're not done!"

"I know I'm not done," I reassured them. "I'm just going to continue working on myself while living in the California sunshine. I have some money left over from the sale of my house. I'm going to go."

"Do you have a plan?" one of the therapists asked.

"I'm going to meet my daughter Sharrin in San Diego for her spring vacation. I'll rent a car, and we'll explore La Jolla and look for a place for me to rent. I loved Black's Beach when I was in California eight years ago, and I'd rather spend the summer there than go back to Fire Island." I'd spent the last five summers there in Kismet, the singles town for the over-forty crowd. "I'm done with 'sex, drugs and rock & roll,'" I announced. "I'm ready to move on."

"What does 'moving on' mean to you?" asked the other therapist.

"Well, I can't explain it, but . . . it's been two and a half years since I left the school and came to the Institute for this inner journey. I intended to start a corporate career in the city as a human resource director. But now I realize I don't want to work so hard. I want an easier life in the sunshine."

"So, you want to become a full-time beach bum."

"No, not full-time. I feel a calling to CSP."

"What's CSP?"

"Center for Studies of the Person. It's an organization in La Jolla that was founded by Carl Rogers and others. He's a world-famous psychologist, and I loved all of his books. He expresses who I am and what I believe. He writes about being genuine, trusting in oneself, being empathic and accepting others. Rogers' person-centered approach helps you listen to your own inner voice. Mine is telling me to connect with CSP.

The La Jolla Program was a CSP program, and it changed my life."

Eight years earlier, I had enrolled in the La Jolla Program after reading about it in Rogers' 1970 book, *On Encounter Groups*. He described the La Jolla Program as a safe, supportive environment for people to interact, share their experiences, recognize perceptions about themselves, and find creative solutions for personal and interpersonal challenges. The program ran three sessions every summer on the campus of UCSD in La Jolla, California. One hundred people were accepted for each session, and the program was so popular that participants could not re-enroll in future summers. I know because I tried. Participants came from all over the world and then went back to create more humane connections and environments in their personal and professional lives.

When I'd enrolled back in the summer of 1974, my goal had been to learn how to facilitate groups that promoted individual growth and built community. At the simplest level, we were looking for ways to get even the three-, four-, and five-year-olds to participate more responsibly in classroom cleanup. With the faculty, I wanted to create a shared democracy, not an authoritarian director-led model. And in our annual August teacher-training program, I wanted to give public school teachers, as well as our own faculty, the experience of learning in a student-centered open learning environment. I'd enrolled in the La Jolla Program solely for professional reasons, but months later, when I arrived on campus, I was seriously considering leaving my marriage. I learned to facilitate groups nondirectively, but it was the personal stuff that was life changing, I explained to my therapy group. "During a weeklong encounter with an angry guy in one of my La Jolla groups, I came to see that I was blaming Myles for not being involved in our relationship, but I wasn't taking responsibility to ask for what I wanted. I'd never learned to do that growing up. I never made demands or got angry at my parents; it was too dangerous." I reminded the therapy group about my mother's frigid, icy silent treatment and shivered remembering how this had made me feel as a child. And then I changed the subject to warm and wonderful.

"At Black's Beach, I learned how delicious it felt to totally, naturally, freely enjoy the sun and the surf. I was more comfortable as a woman in my body than I had ever been stuffed into a bathing suit trying to hide the fat or look sexy. That was a lot of learning from one seventeen-day program."

"It sounds particularly enticing right now," someone in the group said, "in the middle of a New York frigid February with all the dirty snow piled at every corner."

I nodded. "Yes. Forty-six years of this is enough for me."

"So, are you going to apply for a job with CSP?" someone else asked.

"I don't know how it works," I answered. "I just know I'm going."

"Do you know anyone there?" yet another group member asked.

"Yeah, I do. There was this adorable Long Island kid I took tennis lessons from in Fire Island, Billy. He's out there. He graduated from San Diego State, and now he's living in California permanently."

"What about people from, what did you call it, CSP?"

"To tell you the truth, when I was there eight years ago, I

didn't make a connection with any CSP people. I spent all my free time going to Black's Beach and playing with a guy named Andre, an adorable French guy. Never in my wildest dreams did I think I might move out there. But now, well, now, I'm just gonna do it. To start, I guess I'll take a lot of tennis lessons from Billy," I said, only half-joking. "California, here I come!"

Unlike my move from Tenafly into Manhattan three years earlier, this time, I felt prepared. My therapist, Judith, had worked with me. She guided me on a visualization of the condo (with an ocean view) I wished to manifest. She also had me pick a tree in Central Park and hug it, a concrete reminder to "root" myself in nature when I felt lonely or anxious. She even had me envision the tennis lessons with Billy. I discovered that there was another CSP summer program called Living Now that also had small ongoing encounter groups like the La Jolla Program . . . so I enrolled. It would start two weeks after my move. I was ready. Or so I thought.

# MOTORCYCLE MAMA

July 1982

I looked up—way up—for he was over six feet tall. He was holding a motorcycle helmet. I batted my eyelashes and commented, "I've never ridden on a motorcycle."

He took the bait. "Well, maybe when this program is finished, I'll come over and take you for a ride."

"That sounds like fun," I said, quaking inside. Was it my fear of motorcycles or of this gorgeous older man, a long, lanky version of Charlton Heston? Unlike Myles and most of the men and boys I'd ever dated, he was definitely not New York Jewish.

He told me he was a retired physician, an anesthesiologist, and he was a member of CSP. Had I scored big time? I'd moved from New York feeling a "calling" to CSP, but a connection in the form of a sexy older man was not what I had envisioned.

Yet there I was, three weeks into my move to California, standing in a UCSD dormitory lounge, sipping cheap white wine from a plastic cup, going beyond what I had imagined. I had enrolled in this CSP summer program as a first step on my hoped for, but unknown, path toward CSP membership, and during one of the first evening socials, I'd been chatting with Tim, my adorable twenty-four-year-old buddy from my small group, when suddenly he said, "Oh, Suzanne, I'd like you to meet my dad, Ray."

A month later, Ray and I were standing outside my newly rented condo in front of Ray's shiny red BMW bike—of course, it was red—and once again, I found myself looking up at him.

This time, he stood close to buckle the chinstrap on the helmet he'd brought for me. Then he hopped onto the bike and instructed me to do the same, holding on to him and "no jiggling around." That first day we rode up the coast to the Oceanside Marina and back. It was glorious. Despite all my years of warning my daughters to stay off the backs of motorcycles, I felt totally safe.

Ray played it safe too. After hours of sitting with my arms around his waist, feeling all those vibrations of the bike, on fabulous rides out to the mountains of Julian, he dropped me off with nary a kiss goodbye.

After the third or fourth ride, I invited him in for a drink. And so began phase two of our relationship: long, wonderful motorcycle rides followed by long, wonderful conversations sitting on the two high canvas director's chairs on my terrace overlooking the ocean, with the chemistry building but no hint of a move from him.

Finally, one day, I couldn't stand the tension any longer. I got off my chair, walked over to him, and leaned in. And what did he do? He still didn't kiss me. He started blowing in my ear, blowing and blowing until I was ready to jump out of my skin. Instead, we jumped into bed. And so it began.

Once he had me, it was clear that our relationship would be totally on his terms. I was welcome to come along for the ride—or not. I opted in. One evening, I arrived for dinner at Ray's house atop Mount Soledad, and he handed me a sailboat brochure. "What's this?"

"That, my dear, is a Hinckley, the best sailboat in America. I've decided to order one."

"Nice toy."

"Oh, it's more than a toy. It's going to be my home."

"Your home?"

"Yes. I'm going to sell this house and my Cadillac and ride my bike to the Hinckley boatyard in Southwest Harbor, Maine. Then, I'm going to watch them build my dream sailboat, right there at the best boatyard in America. When she's ready, I'm going to sail her down to Mobile Bay. And that's where I'll live, on the boat."

"Wow, big decision. How exciting. When are you going?"

"I'm planning to leave March first."

*Gulp.* "I'd love to ride cross-country with you," I threw out, casually, not admitting to myself or to him that I was stunned by the thought of him disappearing from my life.

The silence felt interminable, but finally he said, "You can come for the ride but then fly home until the boat is ready. Then maybe you can come sail with me sometime."

That's what he said. But that didn't stop me from spinning the cross-country trip on the back of a motorcycle into a romantic fairy tale: living my life on a sailboat, cruising around the Caribbean and maybe the world with this intriguing, sexy older man. That fantasy superseded all of my "professional" scripts about working at CSP.

As we approached departure time, Ray handed me a small molded suitcase that attached to the side of the bike and said, "This is it. What you can fit in here, you can take, nothing more. No purse, no books." I winced.

"If you want to read, every motel room has a Bible . . . as well as a bed."

The bed hooked me. I packed the suitcase with a spare pair of jeans—black corduroy for Galatoire's, the fancy restaurant in New Orleans that had become his hangout as an undergraduate and medical student at Tulane. He said we would stop there for oysters. Before I left New York, I had actually bought a leather jacket at Loehmann's, the big discount women's clothing store in the Bronx, thinking it might be appropriate for San Diego winters. Never had I imagined wearing it for a cross-country motorcycle ride.

It was a glorious star-filled night as we headed east on Highway 8 to El Centro. There was hardly a car on the road. We surmised the whole country was home watching the final episode of *M*A*S*H,* the beloved army surgical unit that was leaving us after eleven seasons on the air. As much as I enjoyed that program, I was more than willing to give up the finale for my own adventure.

My joyful mood continued the next morning as I entered the tacky coffee shop adjoining our motel. I was walking in with Ray, as if we were a couple.

A few days later, leaving a diner in some small town in Texas, we found a crowd of admirers gathered around the bike. I could hardly keep from giggling as we hopped on. I bet they were expecting riders half our age. I was forty-seven and he was sixty-four, but we looked hip in our blue jeans and leather jackets.

I loved the feeling of being in the open air, exposed on a bike, instead of just passing through the environment in a sealed car. I knew when we entered Louisiana without seeing one road sign—I could sense the swampy feel of a nearby bayou. I was seeing the country, even if we were zipping through. However, as we headed up the East Coast, the trouble began. I don't remember if we were in Savannah or Charleston—it was in one of those famous gracious southern towns.

"Could we take a little cruise around the stately homes just to get a feel before heading out?" I asked.

"I'm not here for sightseeing," he retorted. Then he added, "Or stopping in New York City to meet your friends."

"But I thought you were going to stay at Barbara's with me for a few days, so I could show you my city."

"I repeat, I don't want to stop anywhere. I want to head straight north to the boatyard. No distractions."

*Ouch.* He had become a man on a mission once we left his friend's condo in Pensacola. We'd crossed the entire United States from coast to coast, but now as we headed north, he'd had enough of me. All I said was, "Okay, I guess we should find a station where I can catch a train into the city."

I didn't have a purse, but I had my credit card. He dropped me off someplace in Delaware, and I headed into New York, straight to Barbara's. I'd been exhilarated by the cross-country motorcycle ride but then became deflated, maybe even heartbroken, by how it ended.

Talking it all out with Barbara, I could eventually see the gap between my fantasy of romance and adventure and the reality of Ray's single-minded quest in which my role had been, at the most, peripheral. As always, with Barbara's support, I was able to face the truth and make peace with it.

———

I was more than somewhat surprised when, just a few months later, Ray called and invited me to join him, his nephew Rodney, and his buddy Jim, an ex-Navy experienced sailor, on the maiden voyage down the East Coast from the boatyard in Maine. His final destination was Gulfport, Mississippi, on Mobile Bay. The prospect of a new adventure banished the memory of how things had ended back in Delaware; excitement overwhelmed reason. Just as I had been a passenger on the back of his motorcycle, so I became a passenger in the cockpit and the bunk of his sailboat. I told myself: *See, he really does value me.*

The first night out was exquisite. I sat in wonder, mesmerized by the star-filled sky and the lapping of water. Then suddenly a storm came up, and the boat began tossing and turning. Young Rodney, brought along for brawn, spent the entire storm hanging over the side railing, vomiting. Ordered to "stay put," I sat huddled in the opposite corner with the rain and the wind blowing in my face and the boat bouncing up and down and maybe sideways too. I wouldn't have dared to move anyway, for fear of falling—not just falling down but falling off. Eventually, it stopped. Either it blew off or we sailed out from under.

We sailed down the New England coast and then, late one afternoon, on a perfect calm, clear day, we entered the East River of New York. I was sitting alone on the bow of the boat as we sailed right past my parents' apartment building on Sutton Place. In disbelief, I looked up eighteen stories to the first setback, and stared at that terrace where, less than three years earlier, I had felt so alone as I went through my deep inner journey in therapy while I lived alone in that apartment.

We sailed past the UN, under the Brooklyn Bridge, and out into New York Harbor, straight past the Statue of Liberty. I was in awe. All four of my grandparents had arrived alone, in steerage as immigrants, only ninety-odd years before. And here I was sailing by Lady Liberty on the bow of a private yacht. It was the peak experience of the trip—and one of the highlights of my life.

However, living with Ray was not easy. He was the captain of the ship twenty-four hours a day, barking commands at me—in bed and out. I began bristling at behaviors I'd accepted at the start. By the time we got to Florida, I was fighting back against his need for control. As we approached Fort Lauderdale, he announced, "It's time for you to get off the boat."

I gulped, then replied, "That sounds like an order. If that's how decisions are going to be made in this relationship—unilaterally—then I'm out of here—the boat and the relationship."

I realized there would be no partnership with Ray. He talked the talk of mutuality, but he did not walk the walk. I knew I didn't want into be a mere passenger in his life. The question was, what *did* I want?

# ZIGZAG

Fall 1985

I swiveled onto a stool and ordered my now standard California drink: a glass of chardonnay. When the bartender disappeared to the far end of the bar, I scanned the room, but didn't see any prospects for a chat, much less for a sexual adventure. So, I settled back and let my thoughts wander . . . *What's in store for me here?*

Suddenly, my attention was riveted. There, parading before me was a silent procession of people in single file, all in saffron robes draped over one shoulder, some with shaved heads. *Ah,* I smiled, *that's my crowd.* I might have been sitting at a sophisticated LA bar, scanning the room for attractive men, but I was about to join the saffron-robed silent parade. All I could do was giggle!

I'd been exploring new age teachers and Eastern philosophy and spirituality for a while. As I sipped my wine, I thought back to my introduction to new age California and "guru" Terry Cole-Whittaker. She had a big buzz in San Diego; she was a blond California girl, former beauty queen, and successful preacher of prosperity. As I was settling into my new city, Dr. Terry was making big news for leaving the church she had built from fifty to five thousand. She was carrying forth on TV and freelancing around town as a special guest preacher on Sunday mornings. For the challenge of dating, Whittaker offered a neat solution: "Get clear about what you want. Make a list of the ten most important qualities you desire in a partner." So I did.

1. Really intelligent
2. Successful
3. Attractive
4. Personable
5. Sexy
6. Financially comfortable
7. Warm
8. Loving
9. Wanting a relationship

I couldn't come up with #10.

Then Whittaker said, "Meditate on those qualities daily, and you will manifest them." It was relatively easy for me to make my list, and it was clear that Ray did not meet the last three criteria. While I waited for Mr. Right to appear, I continued to explore other spiritual paths.

One such exploration included reading a book by the spiritual teacher Muktananda, the head of the Siddha Yoga lineage. Muktananda had anointed a woman named Gurumayi and her younger brother to jointly take over their lineage when he died. In the Western world, word had it that

Gurumayi, not her brother, had the magic. I was into the movement toward women's empowerment, so I was rooting for Gurumayi. She was who I'd come to LA to "meet."

I got down off my barstool and followed the entourage into a large hotel ballroom where chanting had begun. I had no idea what it meant. There were several hundred people, *maybe five hundred?* It was spellbinding. Then the chanting stopped, and Gurumayi appeared. She was gorgeous. *Was it her physical beauty or her spiritual aura?* I wasn't sure. Throughout the weekend, there was lots of chanting interspersed with dharma talks. During the silent meditations, I sometimes dozed off. I was failing as a meditator. It wasn't easy to stay alert, relaxed, and focused, all at the same time.

As we poured out of the hotel ballroom for our lunch break on Saturday, an adorable curly-haired brunette started chatting with me. She was a psychologist, also from San Diego, and knew some of my female colleagues from CSP. The first question I asked her was, "Where do you get your hair cut? I love it." The conversation flowed effortlessly, and we ended up not only having lunch together but also continuing to meet for every meal during the rest of the weekend.

Was it over dinner Saturday night or breakfast Sunday morning that she asked, "Have you heard about AWP?"

"What's that?"

"The Association for Women in Psychology. The meetings are wonderful. It's so different from the exclusive old boys' club of the APA (American Psychological Association)."

"How? How's it so different?"

"It's a totally different atmosphere. At AWP, women present their work and discuss it in a collaborative rather than competitive way. It's exciting to participate. They're not trying to emulate the medical model to justify themselves like so much of traditional psychology."

"That's one of the things I love about Carl Rogers' work," I said. "He listens instead of prescribing."

"Yes," Catherine agreed. "And the humanistic psychology division of APA is definitely more into research by and about women. But AWP is women only, and it's a lot more fun."

"How?" I asked innocently.

"Honestly? My favorite part is the dance."

My mouth must have fallen open, and my eyes popped as the light went on . . . a women's psychology organization with a dance? *Was Catherine telling me she was a lesbian?* I was embarrassed. It had never occurred to me. I had been so naturally warm and friendly, happy to make a friend in that impersonal ballroom. *Did she think my comment about her haircut was a come-on?* I was embarrassed.

I didn't know what to say, so I awkwardly announced, "One of my daughters is a lesbian."

Catherine smiled and asked, "How do you feel about that?"

"Great." I shrugged. "Sharrin is wonderful. She really knows herself. I love her a lot. We're very close."

When the weekend ended, we exchanged phone numbers to meet for lunch when she was in town. Catherine was a consultant and traveled a lot. Our lunch plans never materialized, but six weeks later, she showed up at a Christmas party at the therapy center of two of my CSP colleagues in southeast San Diego.

From plastic cups, she sipped Perrier while I guzzled

white wine. She stood sideways against the wall with her back to the party, effectively boxing me into a cozy corner that no one else could enter. The air between us was charged. After Ray's "hard to get" narcissism and all the losers I had met from personal ads in the *San Diego Reader*, here was Catherine, leaning in enticingly. "I came tonight hoping to see you."

I flirted back a little. "It's a nice surprise to see you too. I was expecting only CSP members. I like them, but—"

Catherine interrupted, "They're nice, but not a lot of fun, like me."

"Are you?" I shot back.

"Am I what?" she countered.

"A lot of fun?"

"In so many ways," she led on.

"Wanna be more specific?" *Did I really say that?*

Thinking back on my Whittaker list, I realized I had neglected to specify gender. With Catherine, I could check "yes" to every quality I wanted in a partner:

1. Really intelligent
2. Successful
3. Attractive
4. Personable
5. Sexy
6. Financially comfortable
7. Warm
8. Loving
9. Wanting a relationship

*Why not?*

My daughter Sharrin was arriving the next day for Christmas vacation. Catherine said, "Oh, I'd love to meet her," so the three of us went out for dinner. They hit it off immediately and playfully ganged up on me.

"I always thought Mom would make a terrific member of our team." Sharrin wasn't just giving me her blessing—she loved the idea.

"Two against one," I pleaded. "I don't have a chance."

Catherine teased, "I don't know. They say it's dangerous to get mixed up with civilians. Sometimes they change their minds and break your heart."

I sat there smiling as Sharrin said, "When my mom decides to do something, she never second-guesses herself. Did she tell you about the school and the divorce and moving to California?"

I raised an eyebrow at Catherine. "Weren't you once a civilian too? There was that husband you told me about, the father of your kids."

After dinner, Catherine came home with us. Sharrin said goodnight and disappeared. I felt suddenly shy and awkward. Catherine backed me against the wall and kissed me. It felt soft and delicious. She wanted me, and I loved feeling wanted. I admitted to her, "I'm reeling from this, but I like it."

After Sharrin went back to school, Catherine and I spent our evenings together at her house or mine whenever she was in town. Our schedule revolved around her work. We became a couple very quickly. We were discreet when we went out in public, to dinner and the movies. I delightedly told friends, "Guess what? I'm in a relationship—with a woman!"

I said to myself, *Ah, so this is my California chapter.*

Friendships with women had always been important to me. Now, at forty-nine, the added component of a primary relationship with a wonderful woman seemed very appealing. After the failure of my marriage and subsequent romantic relationships with men such as Ray, I was happy to join the lesbian community.

Catherine invited me to an annual lesbian event: a formal dance at a big hotel in LA. I was curious and enthusiastic about going. I asked, of course, "What do they wear?"

"It's 'we,' not 'they,'" she corrected me. "And wait till you see. The range of clothes is fabulous. Lots of tails, which look adorable, and everything else from gowns to sneakers."

"Well, I got rid of my dressy clothes before I left New York. I don't even own a dress. What are you wearing?"

Although she was petite, Catherine almost always wore flowy tops and gauzy skirts. It was her unique signature look. She pulled out an outfit from her closet. It was the same voluminous style, in an ivory color. "Oh," I sprang up. "I've got my creamy Go Silk jumpsuit." I felt elegant and classy when I wore what felt like an expensive man-tailored white silk shirt, its collar left open to the sexy third button and sleeves casually rolled up three times. I had bought it at Barbara's store.

Barbara had moved to California two years after me, and while I was adventuring with Ray and getting involved at CSP, she had opened a fabulous clothing store in La Jolla. "My jumpsuit is my favorite item of clothing," I told Catherine. "I like the way it feels."

"Great," she replied. "We'll look like an elegant couple."

I was excited by the prospect of seeing hundreds of lesbians all in one place, and all dressed up. We drove up from

San Diego and pulled into the hotel entrance. A valet opened my door, and I stepped out, ascended the red-carpeted steps, then turned around to join the crowd of oglers at the top. Catherine gave the valet the keys and then joined me, smiling.

*Oh my God,* I realized as she reached for my hand, *I'm wearing the pants. They'll think I'm the man in this relationship!* That was not how I saw myself. But once we entered the ballroom, my binary male/female stereotypes vanished. There were lots of couples in tails, and Catherine was right—they did look adorable. But there were just as many couples with both women in long, slinky dresses and as many again with one in a dress and the other a suit. My favorite couple stayed on the dance floor for every dance all evening long. They were two late-middle-aged women, rather portly and buxom, dressed in tweed jackets with matching A-line skirts, one in brown, the other gray, both wearing what I guess you'd call sensible walking shoes. One had short hair, the other a bun, and they clearly enjoyed dancing together. They looked straight out of central casting for an eastern prep school headmistress or women's college professor.

Catherine and I had fun dancing and socializing with her friends. We laughed when the band played the first slow dance and we each reached for the other with our right hand up and the left ready to circle each other's waist. Neither of us could do the male lead position, so we happily settled with our arms around each other.

Then, my parents came out for a ten-day visit. I invited Catherine to join us for dinner and introduced her as "my good friend." My friends had always adored my mother and accepted her propensity to give advice as an expression of her genuine interest in them. With Catherine, my mother was more guarded. *Was it because Catherine wasn't Jewish, or did my mother sense something else?* I didn't invite Catherine to join us again, and all parties were probably relieved. I certainly was. My parents had never met any of the men I'd dated before or after Myles, except for a junior rabbi I dated at twenty. I was turning fifty and certainly didn't seek their approval of my social life now. Neither my mother nor I mentioned Catherine again. My dad was oblivious.

Sexually, so long as Catherine came on to me and initiated the way men do, I was happy. I enjoyed the novelty of her softness and curves. I was shy and inept at first, but finally said, "You feel luscious," as I hesitantly caressed her breast. I was fascinated to see how the female body looked from the bottom up. It didn't come naturally to be the giver rather than the receiver of female pleasure. I complained, "I can't believe how hard it is to find the magic button."

I think she enjoyed the role of teacher. However, the first time she strapped on a dildo I freaked at the sight of male and female parts on the same body. When she said, "Your turn," I could not reciprocate wearing the dildo. Maybe that's when the trouble began. Or maybe it was just symbolic of my dawning discovery that I was fine with being a lesbian socially, but my basic wiring was heterosexual, and I liked it that way. I loved being an active participant sexually, but I wanted to be stroked and entered as a female.

Outside of the bedroom, I did not want to play "wifey" or be dominated by Catherine, with her wants taking precedence over mine. I had been raised to be a wife and rebelled against it once. Now, I started to feel myself falling into my old familiar habit—being the supportive partner, with her agenda taking precedence over mine.

Over time, a light began to dawn. I didn't want to wear the pants, but I didn't want Catherine wearing them either— except sexually. Not only was I not a lesbian, I didn't want to be in a relationship at all. I wanted to be a single independent woman, not a partner. Like Ray, I wanted to be the captain of my own ship. I didn't know what lay ahead, but regardless of whether it would be smooth sailing or choppy seas, I wanted to steer my own course.

# PART II

—

## My 50s
## SHINING

# DESTINY CALLS

February 1986

"Hello, Suzanne. This is Carl Rogers calling."

I gulped. During the almost four years since I'd moved to California and become a member of the Center for Studies of the Person, Carl Rogers (CSP's world-renowned founder) hadn't been around much. He had been off doing peace work around the globe. His illumination of empathy, acceptance, and genuineness as the core conditions of a helping relationship had become an integral part of current practice in psychology and many other fields. Recently he had been using what he'd learned about group processes and conflict resolution to facilitate peace in international hot spots.

"I'm calling to interview you," said Rogers.

"Oh *(gulp)* . . . okay," I said. *Pause. Gulp. Silence.* "About a forum?" I asked, feigning casualness.

"Exactly. Maria tells me that the idea of putting on an international forum in La Jolla came up at CSP's retreat last week." Maria was Maria Bowen, one of the co-founders of CSP with Rogers. I had joined her women's group a couple of years earlier, and we had become close personal friends. "I like the idea of an international meeting, but, frankly, I have misgivings about CSP's ability to pull it off. Maria tells me you have organizing experience, so she recommended I call and check you out for myself."

*There it is, I thought—the person-centered approach. He's being open, genuine, and non-directive, just like in his books.* I began telling him about my experiences, starting out as a parent volunteer at a Montessori nursery school and creating the American Montessori teacher training program, then founding my own school.

"I think that organizing and administering a forum might be somewhat similar to my experience organizing the Montessori teacher training program. I worked with the training committee and translated their ideas into an operational program, and I enrolled teachers and collaborated with schools around the country."

He asked relevant questions like, "What was the size of your program? What role did you play? How many people helped you?"

I answered his questions, then said, "Actually, when I left Montessori and started my own school, you helped too. You published your book *Freedom to Learn* the year after we opened, and that book validated everything we were doing at the school. I created the Center for Open Education as a student-centered school and teacher training center." I paused, but Carl didn't say anything, so I continued, "But my leadership as a person-centered administrator really evolved after I took the La Jolla Program in 1974. I learned a lot about building community. I think it would be wonderful to organize the

NAKED AT THE HELM

forum, not only as an international meeting but also as a community-building activity for CSP. It's an opportunity to get all the members involved."

"Do you think you could do that?"

Without hesitation, I replied, "Yes, I do. And at the CSP retreat, there seemed to be lots of enthusiasm for the project."

"It's not my decision alone, but as far as I'm concerned, you're hired!"

I was thrilled. I had moved out to California feeling the call to CSP with no idea what I would do. Now, at fifty, I had a job offer that was a great match for the envisioning and organizing skill set I had developed in my previous career in education. I was off and running in a new career.

# MIRROR, MIRROR

Summer 1986

*Where am I going to sit? It's so crowded already.* About sixty people were squeezing into the lounge on the top floor of Tenaya Hall, a tall, modern gray dormitory at the edge of the UCSD campus on Torrey Pines Road. I headed toward a seat with a great view looking west all the way to the Pacific Ocean. *Wait,* I told myself, y*ou're on the staff. You should take a seat with your back to the light, so you can see faces better.* The lounge couches were already full, and I knew my back would get too sore if I sat on the floor, so I settled into a fiberglass chair at the far end of the circle. We were assembling for the daily community meeting of all the participants in the Living Now program. I smiled to myself, enjoying the fact that I was going to be working in the La Jolla Program too. In fact, I had been a facilitator at the La Jolla Program for two summers and was now a permanent member of the four-person La Jolla Program team. There was a subtle competition between the two CSP summer programs, and I was the only CSP member who had ever been invited to be on both faculties. Again, I smiled to myself; along with my job as coordinator of the international forum, my "calling" to CSP was certainly being fulfilled.

Gay Swenson, the co-director of Living Now, greeted the community, then artfully segued into a mini-lecture on the core conditions of the helping relationship: empathy, congruence, and unconditional positive regard. I tuned out, thinking instead about how important Living Now had been in my transition when I had moved from New York to California four years earlier.

Back in April of 1982, less than three months before my move, a New York friend received a CSP Living Now brochure in her corporate mailbox in the personnel department at the New York headquarters of a multinational bank. Knowing my moving plans, she forwarded the flyer to me. Receiving that mail was an "aha" moment for me, an affirmation of my inner voice leading me to CSP. I knew Carl Rogers was based at CSP, but I didn't know who Rogers' colleagues were or what else CSP did, except for the La Jolla Program. When I'd taken the La Jolla Program eight years earlier, no one there had mentioned that CSP also offered this other summer program, Living Now. Though I hadn't heard of Living Now until I received the brochure, it offered a concrete way for me to make a connection to CSP, so I enrolled immediately. It was reassuring to know that if no one talked to me during my first two weeks in California, I would enter a welcoming place at CSP's Living Now program on July 15.

When I told Barbara I had enrolled, her response was, "Suzy, you've been facilitating groups at the school and doing lots of other training in humanistic psychology for eight years, why would you enroll in a CSP program now?"

"To meet CSP people and hopefully find a way to become a member. But also, I have something I want to learn. I've perfected my skills in facilitating small groups, but I still freeze when I'm in a large group. I'm not myself. I want to get as comfortable expressing myself in large groups as I am in small ones, and Living Now sounds like the perfect place to start."

Now, here I was, four years later, a member of CSP and on the Living Now faculty. As I looked around the circle, I remembered how nervous I'd been four years earlier. I'd hardly heard what people were saying until I found a way to break in and introduce myself in the large group.

As I returned to the present, one after another of this year's participants were expressing warm, fuzzy feelings:

"I feel so heard."

"I feel so understood."

"Everybody is so caring."

"Everybody is so open."

Across the room, a woman spoke up: "Not everybody. I, for one, am bored. I think everyone is being superficial."

*Wow,* I thought. *That was courageous! Who is this gutsy woman?*

At the break, I headed toward her. She had a striking appearance, with short auburn hair, sparkling eyes, a big smile, and an effortless-looking European chic style. She was in her late thirties, I guessed, with a Crocodile Dundee–type Australian sun hat hanging between her tanned, well-toned shoulders.

"Hi, I'm Suzanne. I appreciated your gutsiness," I said with a smile.

"I'm Leyla Navarro," she said. I couldn't place her accent. "I'm from Istanbul."

My eyes opened wide. Italy and Greece were the eastern-most border of my international travels; Istanbul seemed exotic to me.

"How long did it take to fly here?" I asked.

"It was a long trip, but I like to get away, so I don't mind. Anyway, I'm taking the La Jolla Program too, so I'll be here for a month."

"That's great. I'm working as a facilitator in both programs, so we'll have plenty of time to get to know each other."

On breaks between sessions, I often hung out with Leyla and an international group on the outdoor deck of a coffee house in the midst of a eucalyptus grove on campus. In some ways I was in awe of Leyla, starting with her courage to speak out in the group with a contrary view. I said to myself, *I'd never have the courage to do that!* I also admired her international insouciance. She made it seem like no big deal that she traveled internationally by herself to take training programs in psychology. I had come to La Jolla by myself twelve years earlier, and I had traveled to Spain alone nine years ago, but I judged my ventures as false bravado, whereas Leyla seemed so comfortable with it all. When it came to courage, I did not, at the time, see myself looking into the mirror when I looked at Leyla.

However, we quickly discovered we had a lot in common. Though she was born, raised, and educated in Istanbul, and I in New York, I was surprised to learn she was Jewish. I had never met anyone from Turkey before and assumed she was Muslim. Then, we discovered, among all the thousands of colleges in the US, her two daughters were attending Brandeis and Bard, the schools from which two of my daughters had graduated.

When we were alone, Leyla and I shared deeply. I told her about my experience leaving Myles and taking the La Jolla Program twelve years earlier. We talked about the struggle between the woman yearning to fly free and find romance and the devoted mother who wanted the security of marriage and family life. I saw my younger self in her. She appreciated being understood. We became fast friends.

At the end of her month in California, Leyla asked me to lead a La Jolla Program in Istanbul the following summer. I agreed on the spot. When I had felt a calling to CSP, California had been a foreign land. *Now Istanbul?* Nude beaches and sex clubs had been "wild" experiences. International friendships and professional experiences were to become so much more nourishing.

# LIGHTS ON

September 1986

I steeled myself as I walked into the dining room of the International House at the University of Chicago. Gray linoleum floor, gray Formica-topped tables, and there, in the center of the hall, a group of maybe eight gray-haired men. They blended into the surroundings in terms of color, but they stood out because no one else was sitting near them. They were the dominant energy in the room.

In the past, I probably would have walked over to the table closest to the door or to any of the twenty or so other individuals and small clusters and politely asked, "May I join you?" but I straightened up, took a deep breath, and marched right up to the power group gathered in the center of the room. I stuck out my hand and said, "Hello, I'm Suzanne Spector from CSP." Though I acted confident, as if I belonged, I was quaking on the inside.

I'd guessed correctly. These were the "old-timers" who'd been with Rogers early in his career, mostly at the University of Chicago. These were the men who Carl had eventually left behind when he departed academia twenty years earlier to move to La Jolla. They were primarily professors of psychology at universities in the East and Midwest. I'd heard or read some of their names. A few had tried joining CSP one way or another, but I knew from my fellow CSP members that the connections hadn't worked and there were scars remaining.

Rogers' ideas were taught in psychology departments, counseling programs, and schools of education, nursing, social work, and business around the country and the world. But, other than CSP, there hadn't been a central nonprofit organization or major academic institution in the US promoting research and training in the person-centered approach. The "old-timers" had just formed this new national organization called the ADPCA (Association for the Development of the Person-Centered Approach), and I was there in Chicago at their first meeting with an agenda. I wanted to make sure they didn't decide to schedule a second ADPCA meeting that might compete with the International PCA Forum that CSP was hosting the following summer.

The next morning, when I arrived for the community meeting, the conference room was already two-thirds full. Maybe eighty chairs had been set up in concentric circles, starting with a dozen in a tight circle at the core that were mostly filled by the "luminaries" I had met when I arrived. That was fine with me; I didn't want to be in the center of things. I was curious to get the lay of the land, to see how large unstructured groups operated outside of the CSP orbit where the person-centered group process had first been developed and studied by Rogers and some of my CSP colleagues. I took a seat and looked around. There appeared to be a lot of Chicago folks who knew each other. I heard lots of Midwestern accents. One woman caught my attention. She kept tossing her long dark hair over her shoulder like an ingenue, though she looked far too old for the role. More like a queen bee, I guessed.

One of the "old-timers" introduced himself and welcomed us all. If I remember correctly, there were no microphones—the room was small enough and pretty tightly packed. One after another, people introduced themselves, then said where they were from, something about the work they did, and why they were here. "I'm the only person-centered member of my department, so I'm excited to be here with like-minded people," was a frequent refrain, which made me appreciate how lucky I was to be part of the CSP participatory community.

Suddenly, one of the East Coast academics made a derogatory slur about the "touchy-feely West Coast types."

With a confidence that surprised me, I spoke right up. "I, in fact, deliberately moved from the East to the West Coast to join CSP, and what I found is that just because we, in the West, deal with feelings, it doesn't mean we check our brains at the door."

I didn't know as I plunged into my response that Carl Rogers was also in the room. When we broke for lunch, he came up to me and said, "I'm so proud to be a member of CSP with you. You are a new shining light in the CSP community."

It is a compliment I will always cherish. Carl was correct—my light, which had dimmed during my last few years at the school and gone dark as I went through my therapy journey, was lit again and glowing ever more brightly.

# GETTING PERSPECTIVE

September 1986

I stared out the airplane window on my return from the ADPCA meeting in Chicago and realized I was no longer a New Yorker; I was on my way home to San Diego and to the Center for Studies of the Person. I reviewed the journey I'd been on since I'd first read Carl Rogers' book *On Encounter Groups* back in 1974. Rogers described the La Jolla Program and recommended it for those wanting experience in facilitating groups that promoted individual growth and built community. Little did I know that the La Jolla Program would become the catalyst for changing my life. But eight years later, when I'd felt the calling to CSP, I'd moved to San Diego, began participating in the CSP Living Now program, and gotten friendly with its directors, Gay Swenson and Nel Kandel, who eventually proposed me for CSP membership.

Adventure distracted me that first year, but when I returned from my cross-country motorcycle jaunt, I settled in as a member of CSP. When Bruce Meador invited me to join the faculty of the La Jolla Program, I was elated. Bruce, my friend Maria Bowen, and others were founders of CSP with Rogers in 1968, the same year I had started the Children's Center. Humanistic psychology had clearly been in the air on both coasts, but it took me a while to internalize that I'd been a pioneer too.

As I leaned back in my plane seat and calmly stared at the endless blue sky, I remembered how tense I'd been two years earlier, in August of 1984, when I stepped off the elevator in Tenaya Hall, at UCSD. It was the opening social of my first La Jolla Program as a member of the faculty. My stomach was fluttering full blast. I figured if I was nervous, the participants probably were too, so I took a deep breath and pushed myself to move about the dormitory lounge, engaging people in small talk: "Where are you from? What do you do?" Suddenly, a curly-haired woman with a heavy New York accent accosted me.

"Are you THE Suzy Spector from the Center for Open Education in New Jersey?" she asked.

My eyebrows arched, and I straightened my back. "Yes, I *was* that Suzy Spector," I replied. "Now I'm Suzanne. I decided to start using my grown-up name when I moved to California. Who are you? And how did you know that about me?"

"I'm Sandy Chamson, and I was a school psychologist in Hackensack. You and your school had a great reputation. I even referred students to you, and they all did well. I'd heard you left the Center, but I didn't know you'd come to CSP. That's something I've thought of doing. You moved from one Center to another Center," she quipped with a little smile. "Does it get confusing?"

"No, some people do refer to this as "the Center," but I call it CSP to keep my Centers straight."

In less than five minutes of chatting with Sandy, I slipped right back full force into the New York accent I had so assiduously been trying to lose. On the positive side, Sandy's reminder of my history gave me a boost of confidence. I had been facilitating person-centered faculty and teacher training groups for eight years, since I'd first taken the La Jolla Program. I didn't need to be nervous.

Nevertheless, that first summer, I asked Bruce after each session, "Am I facilitating 'the La Jolla Program way'?" Over and over again, he assured me, "You're doing fine. Just be yourself."

On my flight home from Chicago, I thought about my journey from the Center for Open Education to the Center for Studies of the Person, from La Jolla Program "student" to La Jolla Program faculty, and now, Living Now faculty as well. I realized that Bruce's advice to "just be yourself" was, of course, the essence of the person-centered approach. I gained a lot more confidence in myself as a facilitator of these open-ended and free-wheeling person-centered encounter groups. My guiding principle was that I was there to facilitate the process by listening attentively and doing my best to create an empathic environment in which others could feel heard, understood, and empowered.

As the plane descended in San Diego, I realized I had changed both as a professional and as a person. I had been scared to walk into that dining hall at the ADPCA meeting, but I did it. And then, when I spoke out in that first meeting, I wasn't scared at all. I just did it. Something switched. The first time, I forced myself; the second time, it was just me. What a long way I'd come from that plane ride to Spain when

I'd driven myself to be the "happy, young divorcée." *Was that only nine years ago?*

I realized with surprise, even shock, that something else had changed. I had just been through three rather intimate group experiences in Living Now, the La Jolla Program, and ADPCA, and not once had I scanned the room looking for an attractive man. That radar hadn't been turned on. *Had I truly become the captain of my own ship?*

When I descended from that plane from Chicago, I was fifty years old, and I claimed a new confidence to be my authentic self. How that would play out moving forward, I had no clear idea. But I had an International PCA Forum to coordinate, and I had invitations to work in Istanbul and Rome.

Was the possibility of an international career unfolding? It felt utterly surprising, yet organic, like puzzle pieces were coming together in ways I couldn't yet fathom. It had been such a leap to move from New York to California. My trips to Greece and Spain had been wonderful adventures for me as a tourist, but I never envisioned deeper international connections. My "inner voice" had called me to CSP, and I had listened, with no vision beyond a California condo with an ocean view and a vague sense of connection to CSP. I couldn't yet see a larger picture of what this new international calling would mean, but I was open, excited, and along for the ride.

# BUON GIORNO

November 1986

I hoped my smile masked the nervous flutter in my stomach as I looked around the circle of twenty or so chattering young Italians. I was in Rome at a training institute for psychologists—my first international person-centered training gig.

Elettra sat next to me. She was blond, middle-aged, and so fluent in English I didn't need to slow down when I talked to her, as I did with most non-native English speakers I met. She was the teacher of this class of prospective psychologists, but for the next five days, I would be "the teacher" and she, my translator as I facilitated the group in a person-centered, nondirective way.

By this point in their training, the participants were all familiar with Rogers' elucidation of the core conditions of a helping relationship—empathy, genuineness, and acceptance. It was my intent to embody those conditions in my interactions with them, to bring the theoretical to life, and to model this way of being. I knew from my own life experience, the more insight and awareness I gained into my own psyche and behavior, the better I was able to engage with others in ways that might be facilitative and therapeutic. I hoped our work would help this group of prospective therapists gain personal insight. My goal was to model a genuine way of being, not to teach them techniques.

A hush descended in the conference room as Alfonso, the director of the Institute, entered, walked over, and gave me a kiss on both cheeks. With wavy black hair and a well-manicured mustache, he looked quintessentially Italian. Alfonso spoke hesitant English and clearly preferred to speak Italian. He directed Elettra to translate for him.

I had met the two of them three months earlier when they attended the La Jolla Program in California, never imagining that the relationships I made that summer of 1986 would lead to lifelong friendships and travel. I had chatted with Elettra and Alfonso during breaks and introduced them to others to make them feel welcome. Near the end of the program, Alfonso came up to me, dragging Elettra with him, and ordered, "Ask her."

"You said you were coming to Italy in November to visit one of your daughters," said Elettra. "Alfonso would like to invite you to visit our program, and I would like to invite you to stay with me in Rome."

I restrained my impulse to shriek, "Yes!" immediately and asked, "What do you mean by 'visit' your program?"

"I'd love our students to experience you as a facilitator. Then they'd really see how wonderful the person-centered approach is," exclaimed Elettra, without bothering to translate for Alfonso.

"I'd be happy to work with your students," I replied. "But,"

I gulped and turned to Alfonso, "I would need to be paid."

While they consulted in Italian, my head was spinning. I'd just come into my own at CSP over the past year. Was I really going to be invited to work abroad like Maria and Carl and some of the other CSP members?

Clearly, Elettra was saying more to Alfonso than simply translating what I'd just said. I later understood she was negotiating for me, telling Alfonso he was getting a bargain since he didn't have to pay my transatlantic plane fare as I was already coming to visit my daughter Sharrin, who was spending part of her junior year in Florence.

Whatever it was she had said, it had worked, and now here I was, in Rome, excited and nervous. I tried to take deep, quiet breaths while Alfonso, with Elettra translating, introduced me to the group of young men and women. I started by telling them the truth—well, part of the truth; I omitted that this was my first time training psychologists outside of CSP. Though the novelty of this international experience scared me a bit, I'd been reminding myself of my years facilitating groups at the school and the deep work I'd done in my own therapy which had unclogged my filters, leaving me freer to be open and present with others.

"I am delighted to be here," I said. "If I were given a choice of all the countries in the world to visit, Italy would be my first choice. I am really looking forward to being with you this week. I must be Italian at heart, because, as you will see, I cannot stop talking with my hands."

The group laughed almost immediately. Elettra's translation was so seamless that I forgot I was being translated. She spoiled me for all future translators because, from the start, she and I had an easy rhythm. By the end of the week, we had bonded in an incredible way. "You were a great translator," I said. "I trusted completely that you 'got' everything I was trying to say."

As we drove off in Elettra's small blue Fiat after the first day, she was bubbling over. "It was thrilling. Translating you, I got to say out loud so many things I've thought as a facilitator but didn't ever say aloud. I thought the 'rule' was that the facilitator remained a blank slate and didn't share her own feelings. But you interacted with group members in such a real way. I was surprised when you said to Giovanna, 'When you were talking about your daughter cutting you off, it made me think of how hurt and powerless I feel when one of my daughters cuts me off. When she tells me how busy and tired she is, and then seems in a hurry to get off the phone, I feel helpless and frustrated. I wonder how you feel?' I was amazed you said something so personal about your relationship with your daughter and how she makes you feel."

"Yes," I replied. "I wanted to let Giovanna know that I empathized, but I was careful not to shift the focus from her to me."

"Speaking your words," said Elettra, "I had the courage to be me."

I smiled. This was the very essence of what the person-centered approach was all about: the courage to be oneself. I felt terrific that I'd had that impact on Elettra. I told her, "It's not that there are prescriptions for how to be a person-centered facilitator; my guideline for myself in that role is basically to convey acceptance and empathy, while being honest about what I'm feeling. What Rogers calls *congruence*, I call *being real*. And I remember that I am there to facilitate, not to do my own work."

"Aha," Elettra said as she pulled the Fiat halfway onto the cobblestone sidewalk. "A parking space."

"Is this legal?" I asked.

She shrugged. "It will be fine. This is Rome."

She linked her arm in mine as we walked along the narrow street, swerving this way and that between other cars parked haphazardly like hers. We joined the early evening parade of pedestrians wending their way home or to the shops along the way.

We reached the end of the street, and I caught my breath. The dimming sun cast a pinkish glow across an enormous square. As I glanced from side to side trying to take it all in, my dear guide informed me, "This was an ancient stadium. It dates back to the first century. It's the Piazza Navona."

"The first century! Wow! But this doesn't look like the ancient ruins. It's so alive. What's that in the center with the obelisk and the big fountain? It looks like the people are doing a circle dance around and around it."

"Ah. The *passeggiata*, the evening promenade. This is why I brought you here at this hour."

"In New York this would be rush hour, but people here are strolling, not dashing or pushing or shoving. It feels quite enchanting."

She gave my arm a squeeze, and we crossed the cobblestones toward the center. "There," she said, with a dramatic wave of her hand, "is the Fontana dei Quattro Fiumi."

As we neared the fountain, I heard the gurgling and splashing of the water, and, seeing the monumental muscled

NAKED AT THE HELM

male statues representing each of the four rivers, I stopped in my tracks. "I remember this!" I exclaimed. "This gorgeous fountain is by Bernini. I studied him in art history at Barnard. I was here on my honeymoon. We were here at midday, and it was hot as hell. I threw three coins in the fountain, and it worked. I'm back." I fished three coins out of my purse and did it again, saying, "See. I didn't need a man to manifest a return to Rome."

Elettra laughed. "You have the wrong fountain. You need the Trevi Fountain for that wish."

"Let's go to Trevi then," I suggested, but Elettra shook her head. "No, you will come back to Rome, but I'm taking you to a special pizza restaurant for dinner, and then for the best chocolate gelato in all of Rome."

My eyes lit up. "Where's the gelato shop?"

"Right off the square over there," she pointed.

"Let's go now and have dessert before dinner."

"What?" she sputtered, looking at me in disbelief. Then, she smiled and grabbed my arm. "Okay, let's go. This is what I love about you. You're so courageous."

I loved being perceived that way. *Am I?* I asked myself.

I had jumped into a bigger pool, far beyond my wildest dreams when I moved to California. *Where would it lead?*

# SETTING THE TONE

August 1987

I parked my car in the UCSD lot closest to International House, grabbed the tote bag containing my portable office for the week, and, with a deep breath, said to myself, *Okay, Suzy, it's showtime.* After almost a year of planning, it was finally time for CSP to host the Third International PCA Forum. As I wound my way through the university campus, I thought, *You told Carl Rogers organizing a forum would be a good community-building activity for CSP, and it certainly has been.* Everyone at CSP participated in the organizing. We had committees for everything from assembling academic paper presentations and experiential workshops to covering every aspect of logistics. We even had a committee to arrange collaborative meal preparation in a dormitory lounge for those participants who couldn't afford the dining hall fee.

We reserved meeting rooms and dormitories on the campus of UCSD and arranged to use International House as our central hub. The stunning building had a swooped roofline and a glass-fronted main hall that accommodated two hundred people. With its outdoor deck overlooking the ocean, it was much grander than any space on campus we'd ever used for the La Jolla Program or Living Now. People even held weddings and bar mitzvahs there.

Our calendar incorporated the daily non-hierarchical, unstructured community meetings that made PCA forums unusual among professional conferences. We also offered small encounter groups in addition to the fare of traditional professional gatherings: paper presentations, panels, experiential workshops, and topical discussion groups.

As I approached the opening of the big event, I felt satisfied. I had enjoyed facilitating the process to get everyone involved, keeping track of everything, and communicating within CSP and with the participants from the larger world. I hadn't lost my touch as a person-centered administrator. For a moment, I flashed back to my very first experience coordinating a big event, not my wedding (my mother did all that), but the first American Montessori teacher training program, back in 1964 when I was twenty-eight. The night before the hundred teachers were due to arrive on the campus of Fairleigh Dickinson University in New Jersey, my father took our family out for dinner and I cracked the crown off my front tooth eating a lobster, leaving me with a pointy little fang with which to greet the participants the following morning. I was mortified.

I came back to the present, to the UCSD campus and the forum. I ran my tongue around my mouth. Everything was intact.

I felt sad that Rogers would not be there. Soon after his eighty-fifth birthday party in February, he'd gotten out of bed in the middle of the night, fallen, and broken his hip. He survived the surgery but then suffered a heart attack and went into a coma for a few days, just enough time for his family to arrive to say goodbye. At the hospital, I'd told his daughter, Natalie, that I had a mailing ready to go out to person-centered folks around the world with the registration information for the forum. I offered to hold the mailing to include a letter from her to notify people when her dad passed. She asked me to write and sign the letter. Consequently, to many of the 180 people at the forum, I was the face of CSP because my name was on the letter announcing Carl's death.

I knew that Carl would not want to be fetishized in any way at the forum. He would never allow the term "Rogerian" because his whole point was that the capacity for growth is in the person; the therapist's or facilitator's role is to provide relational conditions to foster that growth. In the beginning, he called it client-centered therapy to differentiate this approach from the medical model of the doctor-patient relationship that dominated the field of psychology. As the relevance of Rogers' view blossomed in so many other fields, the more general term "person-centered approach" was adopted.

I entered one of the open glass doors directly into the Great Hall of International House and immediately spotted some of my fellow CSP members, as well as a few of the people I'd met at the ADPCA meeting in Chicago. My strategy had worked. To avoid ADPCA scheduling a competitive event during the forum, I'd invited them to hold the second annual meeting during the latter part of the forum and suggested this would be a way for ADPCA to introduce itself and solicit members from the international community. As the room began to fill up, some people greeted each other with excited chatter as if they were long-lost friends. But there were quite a few silent folks too. Maybe they didn't know anyone? Or maybe they didn't know anyone who spoke their language? I gulped and asked myself, *Okay, what am I going to say?* As my stomach flurried, I was regretting my decision not to write a speech. *Just be yourself, Suzy. Just be yourself.*

Maria Bowen, my closest friend at CSP, was seated in the front row of the circle chatting with someone. She signaled me and patted the empty seat next to her. As I approached, they stopped speaking Portuguese, and Maria introduced me to her friend, Marcia, a fellow Brazilian. In fluent English, Marcia told me there was quite a contingent from their native country. Maria and Carl had run big person-centered encounters in Brazil in the late sixties and seventies, which had spawned a large person-centered community of therapists, educators, and activists throughout Brazil. Marcia invited me to the after-hours party the Brazilians would hold every night in one of the dormitory lounges. She assured me it would be the most fun, with the best music and dancing at the forum. She turned out to be correct.

I looked at my watch and gulped. It was time. I turned on a microphone, took a deep breath, and stood up. I don't remember exactly what I said—a generic, "Hello, everyone. I'm Suzanne Spector. On behalf of all my colleagues at CSP, I'd like to welcome you all. We are really excited to see you and get this forum rolling. We hope you're settled into your rooms and have found the dining hall. This wonderful room will be our main hub for the week, and that includes the deck outside with the ocean view." I mentioned the message board and the bulletin board for announcements of any activities not on the schedule. Then I asked CSP members to stand and said, "We'll be wearing these red necklaces all week, so feel free to accost any of us, and we'll try to help with any questions or problems."

Then, I took another deep breath. "Now that the logistics are out of the way, I'd like to open the forum in a more personal way. I don't remember where I first read, 'What's most personal is most universal.' To me, this is the essence of Carl Rogers' work. I brought this candle from home to light for us tonight. My grandmother brought the candlestick from Russia when she emigrated alone at age sixteen, before the turn of the century. I'd like to light the candle to honor the spirit that brings us all together and connects us."

As I lit that candle, I shared a personal memory of having the honor of lighting the Sabbath candles in the synagogue on Friday nights when I was a girl. Then I looked around the room and said, "This human potential movement that we're all part of in one way and another seems to be leading me back in a spiritual direction. I look forward to learning where it's leading you."

During the week that followed, I got plenty of exercise running around campus taking care of details, but I also managed to meet people personally. I joined an ongoing encounter group that met daily and still remember the psychiatrist from Portugal with whom I particularly resonated in that group. The connection wasn't sexual; it was personal, and it was deep. In the daily large community meeting, I made logistical announcements, but otherwise I participated mostly by listening. This was my introduction to the international world of PCA, and I wanted to get my own sense of it. I was so sorry that Rogers had not lived to experience this gathering, but it was clear the person-centered approach was alive and well in many parts of the world. I was fascinated to hear the similarities and differences in how Rogers' ideas about the core conditions for the realization of human potential were interpreted and practiced by others. For me, at the heart of it all was Rogers' maxim that I had stated as I lit the candle to open the forum: "What's most personal is most universal." What I hadn't said aloud, but had also been thinking, was the corollary "Who I am is enough." The more I accepted myself as I was, the more I grew. The more I told my truth, the more accessible and relatable I seemed to be to others. Was that a paradox? For my generation, everything was about how things looked and keeping up appearances. Now it was about telling the truth, and that worked much better.

# TRAVEL BUDDY

Summer 1989

What was I thinking? Though not an experienced international traveler, I did have New York street smarts. So why was I standing on a street in Rio de Janeiro trying to stuff money down my pants?

Before I'd left for Rio, my Brazilian American friend Maria had warned, "Don't carry a purse. Don't wear ANY jewelry; it might get ripped right off your body." So I'd bought a beige nylon money belt to wear under my clothes, and there I was, standing on a street in broad daylight pulling at the waistband of my pants with one hand, trying to stuff Brazilian currency into my money belt with the other, thinking, *Why didn't I do this before I left the bank?*

My stupidity was even more puzzling because I came to Brazil carrying $3,000 in cash for the organizers of the Fourth International PCA Forum. This was our surplus from the last forum in La Jolla two years earlier. I had wanted to send a check, but Marcia Tassanari, my Brazilian counterpart (whom I had met in La Jolla), had asked me to bring cash instead. She had explained, "Money cannot be safely sent through the banks." As the courier with a money belt full of hundred-dollar bills, I was on edge from the time I left home until I met up with Marcia at the airport in Rio. I've never been so glad to unload cash in my life; when we arrived at her apartment and I turned it over to her, I was so relieved. She told me they'd specifically moved to their current building with a doorman and lots of other security after she, her husband, and their young son had been robbed at gunpoint in their prior house.

I was not alone outside the Rio bank. My new British friend, Anne Newell, was doing the same stupid thing with her money. I had met Anne six days earlier at the forum. Sitting on the floor, across the multi-layered circle of three hundred people, Anne stood out in her bright striped sweater with her striking asymmetrically cut straight black hair falling over one eye. I was relieved to hear her speak English in this circle where Portuguese and Spanish were the primary languages. Multi-language speakers informally translated for those few of us who knew only English.

Anne spoke in a clear, compassionate voice about her experience as a social worker in eastern England. I was moved by how deeply she seemed to care about the work she was doing. Then she translated herself into Spanish. At the end of the meeting, I worked my way through the crowd to introduce myself. We discovered quickly that we had each booked plane tickets to return home from Rio two weeks after the forum, each thinking, *I'm not traveling all the way to Brazil for the forum without getting to see the Amazon.* With delight and great relief, we agreed to travel to the Amazon together. My friend Maria had invited me, Carl Rogers' daughter, Natalie, and a few other Americans to meet her family in Bahia after the Forum and she extended the invitation to Anne, so Anne and I could travel on from there.

In one of the forum meetings, as members of the group were debating the merits of the person-centered approach as compared to other forms of therapy, a burly, vibrant Brazilian man with a jet-black beard raised the question: "Is psychotherapy even relevant in the face of the widespread poverty in Brazil?" Although I'd started working in Istanbul and Rome as a facilitator and trainer, this forum was my first large professional meeting outside of the US, and I was excited to expand my social consciousness. I had grown up in an upper-middle-class bubble, had not traveled widely, and was new to psychology, so I had never really considered that psychotherapy might be a luxury of the middle and upper classes. At the international forum we'd hosted in La Jolla two years before, I had found the Brazilian contingent to be wonderfully hedonistic and free-spirited, leading the dancing and partying every night. Two years later in Brazil, I was getting a broader picture of their culture—one that included compassionate concern for the poor and social inequality along with their passionate celebration of life.

———

One day, I was chatting with a vivacious dark-haired Brazilian woman named Carolina, and I made the comment, "I'm hearing so much about the poverty in Brazil, but I'm not seeing it because we are safely tucked away in this self-contained retreat center." Carolina responded, "If you want to come to Recife after the forum, I'll show you the unvarnished truth of life for many Brazilians." Anne and I agreed that it was a wonderful opportunity, so we booked a crazy flight back from the Amazon that took us from Manaus at night to Brasilia at sunrise, then way north to Recife for lunch and the afternoon with Carolina, arriving in Rio late at night. I would not have spent the money to go on a jaunt like this in the States, but I'd hoped that Carolina's invitation would provide an opportunity to get a fuller sense of Brazil.

We arrived in Recife prepared to see poverty as Carolina had promised. Instead, she came to the airport to pick us up with a car and driver and brought us to her beautiful, gated home, where luncheon was served formally. Her gracious, attractive husband came home from his office to join us for the meal. A whole fish was carried in on a tray so large that it almost filled the length of the table. The fish was accompanied by side dishes of many wonderful traditional Brazilian foods. After the feast, her husband went back to work, and Carolina and her driver took us just one block away from the quiet, elegant, paved tree-lined street on which they lived to a dirt road, vibrant with life, with children running barefoot all over the place. The contrast between the two adjoining streets was remarkable. But that was all we saw. Clearly the driver didn't feel comfortable taking us through the poor neighborhood; he all-too-quickly turned back to the paved facade of the city, past a beautiful cathedral, and then on to the charming town of Orinda, which was filled with art galleries and cafés. I guess it was the driver's job to keep Carolina, and us, as her guests, safe. The result was, in the end, a day that was memorable for our experience of wealth, not poverty.

In the hours we'd spent talking as our riverboat meandered up the Amazon from Manaus, Anne and I found we were on the same page—both divorced women who valued and celebrated our independence from marriage. At that point in my life, other than the trip to Greece with Barbara, the one to Spain by myself, and a few trips for my newly launched career, I had not traveled much internationally on my own. And I very much wanted to become a citizen of the world. I loved participating in the Brazilian forum, and so did Anne. We agreed to attend future international PCA forums together and to plan travel around those meetings. I was thrilled. My best friend Barbara was working and not available for travel, but in Anne, I had manifested an international travel buddy. It was to be the start of a deep friendship, one of several I formed after I moved to California. Over the next fifteen years, we would travel together to twenty countries on five continents.

As Anne and I made our travel pledge, I recalled how during my first year at CSP, a highly cerebral colleague had excitedly shared about a reading she'd had done by a local astrologer. Though skeptical, I'd also wanted to taste all the new age goodies of my new home state, so I'd asked for the name and phone number and made an appointment. When the psychic told me international travel and work was clearly in my chart, I hadn't believed her, but what she'd said was coming to pass. I would spend years wondering about the role of fate in my life; what I did know for certain was that after the good fortune of family, finances, and health, three things played a role: I remained open to new experiences, I trusted my inner voice, and I refused to accept it was ever too late.

# MY WAY

October 1989

At the age of fifty-three, I began a PhD program in psychology at the Union Institute, and from the start, it was an earth-shaking experience. Literally, earth-shaking. My doctoral program began with a required ten-day seminar. These seminars were offered by the Union throughout the year at locations around the country. I chose to begin my program at the conference center in Tiburon, California, and made plans to visit my daughter Donna in nearby San Francisco afterward. I'd heard that Tiburon was charming, on the tip of a peninsula with a gorgeous view of the city across San Francisco Bay. It just so happened that the first day of the seminar was October 17, 1989—a date forever associated with the 6.9 magnitude Loma Prieta earthquake.

When the trembling started, my roommate walked over to the sliding glass door saying, "What's that?" and I commanded in a calm but firm voice, "Get away from there. RIGHT NOW. It's an earthquake."

We continued to feel the tremors and soon thereafter

watched the flames across San Francisco Bay. As my New York roommate prattled on with excitement about her first earthquake, I wanted to tell her to shut up. I was jumpy and tense, hovering by the telephone in those pre–cell phone days; I couldn't reach my daughter Donna in the city. The operator at the conference center couldn't get a call through to any place in the city. I don't know how long I stayed waiting by the phone. It seemed like forever. Finally, the room phone rang. It was my daughter Wendy. "Donna's okay, Mom. She just got through to me in Eureka and asked me to call you because she couldn't reach you across the Bay."

Jubilant that Donna was okay and had only suffered some broken glassware in her charming but somewhat decrepit Victorian walk-up, I joined the group of about twenty adult learners of all ages who looked shockingly relaxed, sprawled around a comfortable conference table for the opening session of our PhD program. Though it took me a while to recover from the worry over my daughter and achieve their level of relaxation, I was delighted to be there.

I'd known about the Union since its founding in the sixties and was thrilled to finally be a consumer of the kind of student-centered education I'd been organizing and facilitating my whole adult life. The Union's external PhD program allowed me to select my own doctoral committee and, with their approval, define what and how and where I was going to study. The Union faculty convener of our seminar was Dr. Penny MacElveen-Hoehn, a tall, attractive woman with long gray-tinged curly hair that she often wore pulled up, then loosely cascading down her back. She seemed about my age, and as a longtime Union faculty member, she shared my orientation toward humanistic education and psychology. Penny and I connected easily from the start, and throughout those first ten days, we ended up taking walks together during the breaks and dining together most evenings. I liked her a lot and asked her to be the Union core faculty member on my doctoral committee.

For the other two professor slots on my committee, I picked Maria Bowen, my close friend and colleague at CSP, and Maureen O'Hara, with whom I wanted to study the psychology of women in classes she was offering in San Diego. Maria had come to America to earn her doctorate in psychology at UC Berkeley and had come to San Diego for a postdoc fellowship with Carl Rogers, which led to the founding of CSP. Maureen had been a member of CSP and had earned her doctorate from Union many years before with Carl Rogers as her mentor. When I took her to lunch to ask her to be on my committee, I confessed to her, "I find your brilliant mind incredibly stimulating, but I'm also intimidated by your intellect. I won't be able to do work like yours."

I have always remembered her answer to me:

"Academics are very good at talking to each other from their ivory towers," she said, "but we need people like you who understand what we are saying, who can then translate us to others and make things happen."

I realized, *Wow, she nailed me. That's exactly who I am.* She saw me more clearly than I'd seen myself. Many times, I've had to remind myself of the me in my mirror when I start judging myself for not being more of a paper-writing original thinker like Maureen or Maria or the women psychologists from Wellesley and Harvard whose work I was devouring. Over and over again, when I started judging myself, I would try to come back to the essence of person-centered psychology—just be who you are.

I found it ironic that I spent the first six months of my self-designed open-inquiry doctoral program totally engaged in old-fashioned rote learning to accomplish what I set as my first task—getting licensed as a clinical social worker. Licensing had not existed when I completed my master's degree at Columbia in 1966. Some years later, when the licensed clinical social worker (LCSW) was instituted, I received a letter offering to grandfather me in, with no requirement more than signing the form and mailing it in with a check. I threw it in the trash, thinking, *I'll never need this. I've become an educator.* And here I was, twenty or so years later, rote memorizing two supersized turquoise loose-leaf binders full of material, covering all that had happened in the social work field since I'd left school. I hadn't lost my cramming/memorizing ability and passed the written licensing exam. However, it took two attempts to master translating my person-centered approach to clients into acceptable cognitive behavioral language in order to pass the oral exam. Colleagues signed off on my hours of individual and group practice, and I received the license that I could have had "for free" if I hadn't been so cavalier many years earlier.

Although the rote-learning component of my program was not intellectually engaging, I was motivated to be "legitimate" as a licensed therapist. The main reason I'd enrolled in the doctoral program was to study the psychology of women in a more focused way than merely reading on my own. Just as I'd said to myself, *Aha, that's me,* when I'd first read Carl

Rogers' *On Becoming a Person* back in 1961, I felt validated again when I studied and discussed the work of Gilligan, Belenky, Miller, and the other Stone Center psychologists who illuminated women's collaborative ways of being as different from the hierarchical, often dominating and competitive male model. When I enrolled in the Union doctoral program, I had no idea of the additional professional surprise that was to come.

# LIFE CALLING, AGAIN

February 1990

Curled up on my couch in my condo in Solana Beach, bored with my LCSW memorizing, I stared at the ocean, then began leafing through the Union catalogue of seminars being offered for the 1990–91 academic year. I was required to take three such seminars as part of my doctoral program. I was totally unprepared for the shiver that went through my body when I read: *Gestalt and Humanistic Psychology Seminar, September 1990, Moscow and Leningrad.*

My heart skipped a beat. I knew—immediately—I was supposed to go.

Three years earlier, Maria had invited me for dinner with her husband, Jack, and Carl Rogers, who had just returned from his first trip to Russia. As we devoured Maria's famous feijoada (Brazilian black bean stew), Carl told us how amazed he was by the reception he had received. Even though millions of copies of his book, *On Becoming a Person*, were sold around the world, and the book was translated into more than a half dozen languages including Chinese and Serbian, it had never been published in Russia.

"I thought there had been a total blackout behind the Iron Curtain, with nothing published on any aspect of Western thought for decades, so I expected to be virtually unknown. I was astounded that the auditorium at the institute was filled with 350 people for my lecture, and then 900 showed up for my public lecture at Moscow University!"

"Wow! How did they know about you?" Jack asked.

"They had read my work from dog-eared underground xeroxed copies of my papers and battered copies of my books that were secretly smuggled in and passed from hand to hand. We sent some material for people to read in advance, and when I asked how many had read it, almost everyone in the auditorium raised a hand. They had even had seminars on it before we arrived!"

Unfortunately, Carl wasn't able to follow up on his momentous Russian visit because three months after his return, he had fallen, broken his hip, and died suddenly.

That day on my couch when I read the Union seminar description, I knew intuitively these were the people in Russia with whom Carl had worked—and I knew I was supposed to go to this seminar and continue that work. For me it was the same sense of calling I'd had about moving to California and joining CSP. In instances both small and large, I heard and trusted my inner voice, without knowing how it was all going to manifest.

This instance was a big one—in September 1990, I found myself in the Gestalt and Humanistic Psychology Seminar in Leningrad, Russia. As we went around the opening circle, I introduced myself as the director of CSP, the Carl Rogers organization, and as soon as we took the first break, one of the

Russian participants came to talk with me. Although he looked quite young, with a shock of brown hair that kept falling into his eyes, Sergei introduced himself as a professor of psychology at the Pedagogical University in Leningrad.

"You said you were with the Rogers organization. Frankly," he confessed, "I'm happy to be here at this Gestalt seminar, but I'm more interested in Rogers' work than in Gestalt psychology. I'm so sorry he died."

We chatted about Rogers and the person-centered approach for a few minutes, and then he asked, "Do you do training?"

I told him I'd been working in Rome and Istanbul as well as La Jolla and other places in the United States. "Did you get to participate in the training group in Moscow with Carl four years ago?" I asked.

"No, I couldn't get in, but I heard all about it from a colleague who actually got into Rogers' small group. He says it changed his life. He's teaching Rogers now and running groups. I'm trying to do that too." Then he looked me right in the eye. "Is there any chance you could come back to Leningrad to do training for us?"

"Yes," I said, nodding. "I will try."

"That's wonderful!" Sergei made no effort to hide his enthusiasm. "Do you really think you can? How soon could you come?"

His enthusiasm was matched by my CSP colleagues back in California. When I explained, "There's an opportunity for a team of us to go back to Leningrad to continue Rogers' work. They can't pay us, and we would each have to pay our own way to get there, but they'll cover all of our expenses while we are there—housing and food. Who wants to go with me?" five colleagues signed on: Maria Bowen, Carl Crider, Shirley Harris, David Meador, and Elsie Zala. I also invited Fran Macy to join our team because he spoke both Russian and the language of humanistic psychology. Fran had been instrumental in arranging the visits to Russia of Carl Rogers, his daughter, Natalie Rogers, who taught person-centered expressive arts therapy, and Virginia Satir, who developed family systems theory. Fran had been the co-leader of the Union seminar, and he and I had developed a special relationship that began when we were both electrified by a performance of the powerful opera *Boris Godunov* at the imperial Kirov Opera House.

Sergei and I began writing slowly back and forth—before the days of email—working out the details for us to offer person-centered training at the Leningrad Pedagogical Institute.

Two months into the planning process, I attended the annual conference of the American Psychological Association in Anaheim, California. APA was the major leagues in professional psychology, and I told myself I should present a paper there as a rite of passage for my PhD. Union wasn't requiring that of me. I was requiring it of myself. Waiting for the allotted time to present my study of single women in their fifties, I found myself alone amongst the several thousand psychologists who were milling around during a mid-morning coffee break. When I overheard a beautiful, willowy young woman speaking what I thought was Russian, I pushed myself to initiate a conversation.

"That sounds like Russian you're speaking. Where are you from?"

She answered in excellent English, "We're from Siberia. Novosibirsk."

"That's a long way to have come. I've never met anyone from Siberia before." I held out my hand. "My name is Suzanne Spector. I'm director of the Carl Rogers organization here in California."

"Hello, Suzanne. My name is Elena Osopova," she replied with a smile.

"Have you heard of Rogers?" I asked as we dropped hands. "He was in Russia in 1986."

Elena shook her head. "I'm a neurologist, not a psychologist, but I'm here as a translator for Dr. M, who is a psychologist. Let me introduce you." She was obviously glad to have someone to speak English with as well as an opportunity to do her job as a translator.

As we both turned to Dr. M, I held out my hand and introduced myself. He shook my hand but did not smile. I continued, trying to engage him. "I'm taking a team to Leningrad next fall to do person-centered training."

Elena translated. He scowled as he said something back to her in Russian. I waited, wondering what he seemed so grumpy about. She translated, "He says, 'You Americans, you only go to Moscow and Leningrad. Nobody ever comes to Novosibirsk.'"

Intrigued at the possibility of traveling to such an exotic spot, I replied, "Well, we would come, if you would arrange it." And arrange it they did! Elena's husband had just started a travel agency, and she was invested in making it a success. Eventually, our plan included three five-day workshops in Leningrad, Novosibirsk, and Tashkent in Uzbekistan. It took an entire year to organize everything. Since they couldn't pay us in currency, our hosts in Siberia offered to take us to Irkutsk and Lake Baikal in eastern Siberia, and our hosts in Tashkent would take us to the ancient Silk Road cities of Samarkand and Bukhara in Uzbekistan. Even Fran, who had been to Russia many times before, had never been to these far-flung places. Sergei took responsibility to arrange for our stay in Moscow to meet with members of the Russian Humanistic Psychology Association at the end of our run and do some sightseeing before flying home.

I was organizing all this slowly, entirely by snail mail, because not only did email not exist, international phone calls were incredibly expensive. In the midst of the planning, Maria encouraged me to attend a theoretical person-centered therapy conference that was being held in Stirling, Scotland, at the beginning of July 1991, two months before our Soviet trip. I wrote to my friend Anne, and she enrolled in the Scotland conference too. Maria presented a brilliant, groundbreaking paper on intuition in the person-centered approach. All of us who were evolving from humanism to a broader spirituality were excited by her work. I had started my doctorate with a desire to expand my understanding and practice of psychology both intellectually and experientially. Maria was a good mentor as well as friend. I convened a discussion group on issues and experiences of people over fifty. By offering a group instead of presenting a paper, I tapped into a desire for experiential participation in that intellectual milieu, even among university professors. I had found my niche midway between the theoretical and the experiential.

At the conference, I also interviewed British women for

my dissertation. I had originally planned to explore the phe-
nomena of happiness and fulfillment in divorced women over
fifty by interviewing American women, but after spending
five days talking to Anne Newell, my British travel companion, in between stops for nature walks and visits to indige-
nous families as we traveled up the Amazon, I was inspired to
have a cross-cultural sample. My qualitative study of single
women in their fifties who were happy subsequently included
Japanese, Russian, and British women, as well as Americans.

I knew Anne would be a wonderful, articulate subject for
my study. She summed up perfectly how so many of us felt in
the 1980s as we entered our fifties as single women and found
what truly made us happy. In my dissertation, I quoted Anne
saying:

"Since entering the crossroads (turning fifty), I've been
on a big inward journey; I've collected up the male and female
bits of myself and brought them together. I feel so alive as a
woman and better with myself than I've ever felt, and I
haven't been in an ongoing relationship with a man for four
years.

"Because I feel complete, I can honestly face the prospect
of celibacy for the rest of my life without feeling, *God, how
terrible*. Before, that would have felt dreadful. I realize that
what I used to look to a man to provide are aspects I have in
myself."

*Wow*, I thought. *That's it. That's what's happened to me.
I've integrated the masculine and feminine aspects of myself.* I
grew up in a family with a strong mother who didn't know
how to show affection, and then I married a man whose sexual
passivity triggered my unconscious doubts about my own at-

tractiveness. I wondered, *Did Myles not want me because I was a strong woman?* "Don't be too smart," was certainly the cultural norm for my generation of women. In that archetypal equation of strong with masculine, a strong woman might be called "a ball-breaker." It took me half a lifetime to integrate my masculine and feminine aspects and accept myself as a strong, powerful, sexual woman.

In our interview, Anne also talked brilliantly about her passion for gardening: "At my cottage in Norfolk, I'm building my garden stone by stone. Following the contours of the land, I planted things between the stones and have the sense of the garden and me working together as the garden evolves, with lots of spontaneity and surprises. As plants reseed themselves, I decide what will stay and what I will pull up."

This was a wonderful metaphor for what many single women in their fifties were doing with their lives. Like most women of our generation, Anne was brought up to please others, especially men, and be an empathic wife and mother. Through therapy and person-centered training, she learned that being honest with herself and congruent in relationships was "probably a more valuable quality than just being empathic." When she spoke of losing her life force in her marriage and feeling dead, it resonated with me completely.

Through flamenco and belly dancing, Anne got in touch with her sensuality and spirituality. She danced to please herself. Anne was such a validating mirror for me—not specifically the belly dancing or gardening—but the core of my evolution as a woman.

After the conference, Maria, Anne, and I piled into Anne's little car for a driving trip across Scotland. Because we were so far north, we were able to go out late into the evening after dinner, tramping through the moors. We were on a quest for ancient sites of female spirituality scattered about the moors of Northern Scotland. Anne had unearthed a small paperback book with a map. We asked local people if they knew of any stone circles. When we finally found them, like three witches of yore, we stood in silence, alone on the moor, holding hands and breathing in the energy of the mysterious circles at our feet.

Less than two months later, I would be dealing with a different sense of unreality.

# THE PINNACLE

August 1991

Late in August 1991, one week before we were to leave for Russia, the old guard in the Soviet government mounted a coup against their reform-minded Communist leader, Mikhail Gorbachev. Regrettably, we all understood our trip would have to be cancelled. I stayed glued to the TV set. I had never followed foreign events so closely. I had never had such a personal investment. From the very beginning when I read about the Gestalt and Humanistic Psychology Seminar in Leningrad, it had felt like a calling—something I was supposed to do, and the idea of not going was inconceivable.

After a week, the coup failed, and a few hours later, my phone rang. It was Sergei. We had never communicated by phone before because of the cost involved. He apologized and expressed deep disappointment that our visit would not be occurring. I interrupted him. "Sergei, we're still willing to proceed with our plans if you want us."

"Really? You'd still come? I am shocked and delighted."

So off we went to what would again be St. Petersburg, a

beautiful city reclaiming its name and imperial glory after decades of being communist Leningrad. Our opening community meeting was one of the high points of my life. There we were, almost one hundred people sitting three- and four-deep in a makeshift circle in a shabby university classroom. The floors were dirty, the lighting was dim, the chairs mismatched—some wood, some metal, some worn upholstery. I don't remember any windows, though they could have just been too dirty to let in any light.

I opened the gathering by saying, "We are so happy to be with you at this moment in your country's history, and we're interested to hear how each of you feels about what just happened." They began pouring out their hearts, speaking of their disappointment and despair when the coup occurred. It was difficult to see faces in the deep circle, but the depth of feeling reverberated throughout the room.

One woman said, in a voice thick with emotion, "When I heard about the coup, I took Gorbachev's picture and hid it in my basement to show to my grandchildren one day. I wanted to be able to tell them about the one brief shining moment of hope and freedom we had in our country under Gorbachev."

Another man said, "When the coup happened, my first worry was about my parents; my second worry was that the Americans wouldn't be able to come."

When I spoke of my joy as I watched Prime Minister Boris Yeltsin in Red Square mounting the tank that turned the tide against the old guard coup, they were in disbelief that I had watched the whole thing on American TV. In St. Petersburg, they had not seen a broadcast of what was happening in Moscow. During their entire lifetimes behind the Iron

Curtain, they had been told untruths about the West, so they were shocked to learn that the rest of the world, particularly America, was interested in them—so interested that American TV was broadcasting live from Red Square in Moscow. They were even more surprised that Americans were actually watching it.

Over the course of the week, we were equally surprised and moved to learn how the human spirit had survived in Russia. Despite being born and raised under a seventy-year-old brutal totalitarian regime, our Russian colleagues expressed a deep and abiding yearning for free self-expression. This consciousness had been nurtured in deep conversations around their kitchen tables and by sharing black market copies of treasured writings by free thinkers. Despite the harsh negation of individuality throughout the Soviet Union, the soul of Dostoyevsky had not been eradicated from their DNA.

As American humanistic psychologists, we were there to help fan that flame of yearning for freedom into a steady blaze, for them and for everyone they touched in their personal and professional lives. It was an honor to be there, to connect with them, and to help facilitate the process of their self-realization. For me, it was the peak experience in my professional life.

On a personal level, we were touched by how generous and thoughtful the Russians were as they hosted us despite the challenges of their daily lives. On the first day, we were struck by how well dressed they were. They wore the same clothes the rest of the week. Without good air circulation in our meeting rooms, by the last day we had a new appreciation for American dry cleaning.

One day, on the bus that transported us from where we lived to where we worked, the driver stopped and disappeared. Sometime later he reappeared laden with loaves of the dark bread we liked, which they had run out of in the dining hall of our dormitory. When we were invited to their homes and served fresh fruits and cakes, we knew they were blowing a month's supply of ration stamps on us. Despite how open they were about personal and professional issues, they never gave us a clear explanation of how the black market system operated that allowed them as professionals to bypass the ubiquitous food lines all over the city.

After a lovely final banquet and a day of sightseeing in St. Petersburg, beautiful Elena, the translator/neurologist I had met in Anaheim, came to St. Petersburg to collect us and bring us to Novosibirsk.

———

"Siberia" conjures up images of gulags and barren, lonely, arctic wasteland, but this was the opposite of what we found upon our arrival at Novosibirsk airport. It was teeming with worn-out travelers sleeping on the floors, awaiting connections. Some looked as if they had camped out for days. We were grateful for Elena's graceful guidance through the chaos.

We learned that, as the third-largest city in Russia, Novosibirsk was a hub for air travel as well as the Trans-Siberian Railway. Interspersed between plain gray Soviet-style buildings were modern edifices, like our hotel, built by a Scandinavian company. The city had none of the imperial grace of St. Petersburg, but the streets, as in St. Petersburg, were peppered by lone babushkas, older women with kerchiefs covering their heads and tied under their chins. They were usually selling beautiful individual dahlias. We were surprised not to see people lined up outside food shops as we had in St. Petersburg, until we realized it was because we had arrived on a Sunday.

When we went to check out our workshop space at the university, we discovered that the central meeting room had been set up with tables and chairs, all lined up and facing forward for lectures and note-taking. Definitely not person-centered. The tables could not be removed from the room, so we pushed them against the four walls and stacked them atop one another. As we started to place chairs in concentric circles, Elena confessed that there might be more than the seventy-five-person limit we had set, maybe closer to one hundred. To squeeze in as many people as possible, we lined up the chairs all facing front in rows—not the interactive circle format we liked to work in, but that was the best we could manage.

Since the city was such a travel hub, 180 people from all over Russia managed to get there to participate in our workshop, many spending a month's salary for transportation and the workshop. We didn't turn anybody away. How could we?

I'll never forget that opening meeting in Novosibirsk. As everyone entered, three of us on the team were sitting on the tables at the front of the room, with the other four team members scattered around the sides and rear. The room filled up—every seat taken. From the back of the room, one of our team members called out, "There are still people outside the door. How can we get them in?"

I replied casually, "In America, we often sit on the floor."

Without hesitation, the people in the front rows of seats gave up their prime spots and moved forward to sit on the hard, dirty floor in front of us. I was so touched. What an amazing sight to behold. Like a snake slithering along, the crowd shifted row by row until everyone was squeezed into the room.

And that's how we began, with this lovely experience of 180 people generously accommodating each other. It was quite moving, literally and figuratively. I wondered to myself, *Would individualistic, competitive, self-centered Americans have been so cooperative?*

I was asked to do a demonstration of person-centered therapy with one person in front of the whole audience. It occurred to me that it had been seventeen years since I first laid eyes on Carl Rogers during a therapy demonstration at the La Jolla Program I'd attended back in 1974. How thrilled I had been that day to be in the presence of "the Master" as he did a therapy session. Now I was in Siberia, being asked to do what I had watched him do, thinking I couldn't agree to do therapy with a crowd watching. I said to myself, *No way, you're not Carl Rogers!* I wish that I had been able to say, *Just be yourself.*

In the end, though I declined to do a demonstration, it happened anyway. Our workshop design had been for our American team to work every day with four small groups of no more than twenty participants. However, since so many people showed up in Siberia and some of my colleagues did not feel comfortable working with small groups of more than twenty, Maria and I agreed to split the balance. In my "small group" of fifty-plus, I was seated in the center of one side of a very elongated oval. I could see the people on the opposite side of the circle from me, but I could not see the faces of those on my side of the room.

On the third morning, a member of the group came in highly agitated. Before the translator could tell me what she was saying, one after another of the Russian participants started bombarding her. There was no time for the translators to translate, but it sounded like they were giving her advice and directions for what to do. They were so excessively talking "at" her, that I also became agitated.

Because of the size and shape of the circle, there was no way for me to make eye contact with her, so I picked up my chair, carried it down the inside of the circle, and sat down right in front of her, tuning out everyone else. There, I asked her what she was experiencing. I then simply listened empathically to what she had to say. I was able to stay totally present with her. The fact that everything she and I said had to be translated slowed down our interaction and actually gave her time to process her feelings. I do not remember what the issue was that she was addressing. I don't think it matters. What was important was that I was sincerely trying to understand what she was feeling, instead of giving her advice.

When she seemed calmer and had some clarity about what she was experiencing, I asked if she felt ready for us to stop. She nodded, and I picked up my chair and went back to my place in the circle. I felt good about the interaction and about myself because I had listened to and followed my own gut, which had said, "Whoa!" as she was being inundated with advice from the group members; my own "performance" fears had disappeared in the face of doing what was right for her.

I returned to my spot and invited the participants to ask me questions and make comments about what they had observed. Someone questioned the "technique" of carrying the chair down the center. With an emphatic shake of my head, I explained, "This was not a 'Rogerian technique,' but merely my way of solving the problem of not being able to make eye contact with a person who was upset and needing an opportunity to explore what she was feeling." I also talked about my own strong urge, in that instance, to intervene. "However," I explained, "in one-to-one therapy, I would probably leave more space for the client to express what she was feeling without interrupting her." I had ended up demonstrating person-centered therapy after all, so it turned into a great teaching moment for the group and a learning experience for me. I recognized, at least in that situation, that who I was was enough.

One night, Elena and her two aides from her husband's travel company drove us through a pitch-black forest in the pouring rain to experience a traditional Siberian banya. Fueled by a good deal of vodka and caviar, first the three men and then the four women on our training team took turns being "beaten" deliciously with branches of laurel leaves, then led, naked, in the dark, for a dip in an icy river. While we were at the banya, I took a wonderful photograph of Maria that captured her draped in a white sheet, looking like a goddess. In all the hours we had spent in vans driving back and forth to our dorms and on the long sightseeing excursions, I'd become concerned about Maria. She had a persistent, unrelenting cough, and I worried she might be seriously ill. Unfortunately, this was confirmed when I accompanied her to the doctor on our return home. Three years later, I would enlarge the goddess photo I took at the banya and display it as the centerpiece at her memorial.

Maria had been a co-founder of CSP with Rogers and others and had been an integral part of all their early international work while I had been running my school and teacher training programs on the East Coast. Working together with her in Russia connected me more directly to the early history of CSP's large encounter groups. Although she was only sixty when she died, she had lived a very full life, emigrating from a family of twelve in Bahia, Brazil, to get her doctorate in psychology, and then becoming a Tibetan Buddhist practitioner and emerging as an intellectual leader in humanistic psychology. I am so grateful we experienced the trip to Russia and Siberia and Uzbekistan together; she was an incredible woman and a significant leader, but I will always remember her as a very dear friend.

# PART III

—

# My 60s
# EXPLORING

# STRIPPING AGAIN

December 1995

*If I strip off my professional identity, what will I find?*

"Suzanne is turning sixty next month. Let's give her a croning ceremony," suggested Judith.

I winced. "Thanks a lot. You say the word 'crone,' and an image of an old hag pops into my head." I looked around our circle of seven women squeezed snugly into Judith's living room. They looked so mellow in the soft flickering glow of the candles we had lit before we meditated. We'd been gathering on the second Sunday of the month for five years for the supposed purpose of nurturing our spiritual development. What we did best was potluck dinners and celebrating milestones.

"Lona, you're older than I am. How do you feel being thought of as an old hag?" I asked.

"No, no, no!" exclaimed Judith. "In feminist spirituality, the Crone is the archetype of the Wise Woman, not the old hag or wicked witch from folk tales."

"Ah, that's better. But that doesn't suit me either. I don't see myself as a Wise Woman."

"Oh, come on, Suzy," chimed in my good friend Liv, who is almost a decade younger than I. "You work and participate in conferences all over the world. You earned your doctorate. You're the director of CSP!"

"Not for long," I muttered.

"What? What did you say?" Liv stammered.

"I've decided to resign from CSP."

"Are you serious? Why?"

"I realized I'm bored. It felt like a calling when I moved here, and it's been great for more than a decade. But now, I'm done. Maybe Maria's death two years ago at sixty has made me wonder what's ahead for me now that I'll be turning sixty. I'm ready for a new chapter."

Saying it out loud made it more real. Leaving CSP and my persona as a humanistic psychologist would leave me, once again, stripped bare, as I had been when I left my marriage and, later, when I left my school. If I wasn't a CSP member, and I wasn't Dr. Suzanne Spector, then who was I?

"You could still have a croning to acknowledge all you've done," suggested Pat.

"No, thanks. Not yet."

"Do you know what you're going to do?"

"I'm so grateful that I own my own condo, and since my father died and my mother is settled here and secure with Isabella to take care of her, I have enough time and money to retire. There are two ways I want to explore in my next chapter. One, I want to travel more. My international friends Anne and Elettra are both single, close to my age, and wanting to travel with me, and Leyla feels like a sister who has made me part of her wonderful family in Turkey.

And, of course, I'll continue going to Santa Fe regularly to visit Barbara. It's still strange that she's not here."

"I miss her too. How long has it been since she went for that summer job in Santa Fe and then decided to stay?" asked Anna.

"She's been gone for two years. Barbara is home to me wherever she is, but I'm grateful I'll have you all as my tribe to come home to from my travels."

"You said you wanted to do two things. What's the other?"

"When I'm home, I want to start exploring a part of my brain I've never used before. I want to take up art. I think that will be an inner leap into the unknown, like going into therapy was way back when. I've taken more outer leaps in my life, like starting a school, moving to California, and traveling internationally. Actually, I'm doing some traveling in two weeks —I'm going to Kauai for New Year's with a Swiss guy I met last summer at a conference in Greece. And I'll probably go to Turkey again next summer. I don't know what else . . . yet."

# SUMMER EMBRACE

July 1996

*How did I get so lucky?*

When I was sixty, my Turkish friend Leyla, her husband, Daniel, and I sat around the shiny varnished table on the stern deck of their spacious wooden sailboat, the *Ergovan*. We were anchored in the Mediterranean, somewhere off the coast of southern Turkey. What was left of our breakfast remained on the table: fresh creamy feta cheese, salty black olives, juicy sliced tomatoes, and crusty white bread, all of which we'd picked up at an outdoor village market the day before. When the mate appeared from the galley, Leyla gave me a big smile. He was carrying the star of the show, her delicious homemade plum jam. I spread a thick layer of the sweet/tart/crunchy/soft confection atop a piece of the fresh bread, admonishing myself, *Only one piece*. While I savored the treat, I reminded myself how pleased I was to be wearing a bikini for the first time in years.

I sat back in the blue canvas deck chair, looked around, and exclaimed, "I feel embraced!"

Daniel looked at me quizzically. "Embraced?" Turkish and French were his first two languages, but he was also fluent in English.

"By the two of you and the captain and mate who take such wonderful care of us, and," I said, spreading my arms out wide, "I feel embraced by the arms of this perfect, tranquil, uninhabited cove where we dropped anchor." As I looked at the clear blue sea, the rocky shore, and pine-filled hills, I exhaled a deep breath of contentment, savoring the moment.

Ever since Daniel had bought this boat (was it seven summers ago?), he and Leyla had invited me to visit them every year in Istanbul; then we flew to the south to sail for a week or two along one or another part of this lovely Turkish coast. In the early days, their three children were with us, even their Dalmatian dog, Jessica. The *Ergovan* was a classic wooden Turkish gulet, a sailboat that I thought of as broad across the beam, with ample hips compared to the sleek schooner I'd sailed on with Ray, my motorcycle man, in my late forties. The gulet design could accommodate six of us at once, stretched out on the bright blue cushions that covered the whole stern of the boat.

After their eldest daughter's wedding, Daniel's sister and her two teenagers joined us on the *Ergovan*, and we sailed in tandem with another gulet they chartered for their other close relatives from Europe and Israel. Except for Daniel, who slept in their cabin, we all used the cabins merely as changing rooms and slept out under the stars. The mate stretched pads across the bow, and we each had our own pillow and light quilt. When Barbara and I had spent the night on the deck of a Greek ferry from Mykonos to Kos back in 1976 fresh out of my marriage, never in my wildest dreams did I imagine I'd be sailing these waters every summer with my wonderful European friends.

As soon as our breakfast dishes were cleared, the captain would direct the mate to crank up the anchor and we would head out to continue cruising along the alluring coastline. While Leyla and Daniel consulted with the captain about our route for the day, I sat down on the padded stern and wiggled my way back from the table until I could lounge against the back pillow with my legs straight out in front of me and my arms stretched out wide. I let out another deep breath, feeling happy and nurtured.

I had fractured my own family life when I divorced Myles, sold the house, and sent my three daughters off to schools and careers. They were now in their thirties, and I mostly saw them individually. To me, our family structure seemed like a wagon wheel; I was at the center with spokes connecting me to each of my daughters, but there was not much connection between them, nor a strong sense of us as a whole. They were busy with their own lives, and family get-togethers were infrequent.

I sank more deeply into the cushions, listened to the lapping of the water against the pebbly shore, and thought about how much Leyla and I were alike, both of us creators of institutions and programs that fostered self-exploration, learning, and growth. When I had met her a decade earlier, she invited me to create a La Jolla Program in Istanbul, and we'd followed that up by creating a training program for Turkish therapists. Perhaps more importantly, she had also invited me into her tightly knit family. I was the friend she could talk to about independence; she was the friend who gave me the family life I had sacrificed on the altar of my independence. I didn't regret my choice to pursue life as the captain of my own ship, but I'd also relished being enfolded in the warmth of her family.

Now their children were living their own lives, and Leyla, Daniel, and I were alone, without family or guests on the boat. Leyla finished her consultation with the captain and suggested, "Let's go sit on the bow and leave Daniel here to read his paper. I'd like to read to you from the manuscript of my new book on women's anger."

We snuggled up next to each other, but before she opened her book, Leyla commented, "We were so busy going out in Istanbul and getting ready for this holiday, we really haven't had much private time. You seem so relaxed now, but when you arrived, I sensed you were upset. Is there something you want to talk about?"

"Yes, actually, there is. I'm looking forward to hearing what you have to say about women and anger in your book. Right now, I'm very angry—with myself. I got into a scary situation in Zurich on my way here."

"What happened?"

"Remember last summer, when you put me on a boat from Turkey to Greece, so I could participate in that person-centered forum in Thessaloniki?"

"Yes, why?"

"Well, I met this Swiss guy, Bruno, at the bar the first night in Greece, and we had a little thing during the forum. Anne's flight was cancelled, so I slept with Bruno that first night. I hadn't had sex in quite a while. It was fun. We walked into town for dinner once or twice, and he held my hand, which was sweet. He also respected that I wanted to hang out with Anne and the other international friends I hadn't seen in three years. Anne was cool about my going off with him sometimes because she and I were going to Santorini together after the forum. Bruno emailed and called me a bit in the fall, and then he invited me to go to Hawaii for New Year's. He came to visit me in San Diego for Christmas, and I took him to a men's shop and got my tailor to do a rush job putting a new lining in his favorite leather jacket. I hadn't done men's shopping like that since my marriage. It was kind of fun. I also took him to see the decorations and hear Christmas carols at the Del Coronado, that beautiful Victorian hotel I took you and Daniel to see when you visited me. Then we flew to Kauai for a week."

"Sounds great."

"Well, it wasn't. On Kauai, he only wanted to go to KFC for a bucket of fried chicken every night for dinner. I don't eat that stuff. He just shrugged and went anyway. It wasn't fun going out to eat by myself. It sure didn't match my fantasy of a romantic Hawaiian vacation. I should have gone home or at least said adios for good at the Honolulu airport.

"But he emailed me this spring and invited me to visit him in Zurich on my way here. I'm mad at myself that I got seduced by the idea of stopping off to visit a European lover for a weekend. I was using an American Airlines mileage ticket, so I landed in Geneva, then took the train to Zurich. I liked the 'story' instead of remembering that I didn't like the guy." I shook my head. "I'm sixty years old. You'd think I'd know better by now."

"Adventure can be seductive."

"Oh, yeah." I nodded. "But it can get you into trouble," I admonished both of us. Then I told her my story.

"I stepped off the train in Zurich feeling excited. The last time a man picked me up at a train station I was a sixteen-year-old senior in high school going to visit my high school boyfriend for a college football weekend at the University of Pennsylvania. This time, though, it wasn't like in the movies. Bruno wasn't waiting for me with open arms on the train platform. I scanned the people waiting, but I didn't see him and got pulled along by the crowd moving toward the station. Finally, I spied him leaning against the wall of the terminal building. He's a big, burly guy with salt-and-pepper hair and matching trim beard, so he was easy to spot.

I waved and gave him a big smile, but he didn't move or come to grab my suitcase; I had to walk up to him. He greeted me matter-of-factly and didn't say a word about my new slim look. I'd lost thirty pounds since I left him in Hawaii after New Year's. I'd expected him to notice!

"He finally took my suitcase, but he didn't put his other arm around me or even take my hand as we walked to his car. On the drive to his apartment, he didn't talk much while I prattled on about the gorgeous train ride through the Alps. Later, I wished I'd paid attention to where we were going. All I remembered was a quiet residential neighborhood with gray stone buildings and some curbside trees. We parked on the street. No one was around. The lobby of the apartment building was dark and wood paneled, and so was the elevator. I didn't notice how many floors there were, what the hallway was like, or how many apartments were on the floor.

"When we entered his apartment, he said, 'Come see the terrace.' I followed him to the far end of the living room. He opened the window and climbed out. Then he turned and gave me a hand. That was the first time he'd touched me, but I didn't think anything of it. The terrace wasn't impressive—a lounge chair and a wrought iron table and chairs with faded cushions. Not much of a view.

"I asked him if he came out there a lot, trying to make conversation.

"He answered, 'Sometimes.' Then he asked if I wanted to stay out there and said that he had to make a phone call.

"I told him, 'No, if you're going in, I'll come back in too.' I wasn't confident I could climb back in without a hand.

"He went to his desk and sat down on the swivel chair, so I walked across the room and sat on the couch. Everything was dark and oversized. From my seat on the couch, I couldn't even reach the big wooden coffee table. He made a call in German, hung up the phone, then stood up and announced, 'I have to go out.'

"It was so strange, but jet lag was rolling over me, so I just surrendered to it. I hardly remember him leaving."

"How weird! How long was he gone?" Leyla asked.

I shook my head. "I don't know, I fell asleep. I'm getting all tense remembering. It's like I'm back there. I awakened suddenly and wondered, *Where am I?* Then I remembered. I looked at my watch. It was six o'clock, but I wasn't sure if that was morning or night. I didn't know how long I'd slept. You know that confusion sometimes when you're traveling?"

Leyla nodded.

I continued. "I wondered, where was he? How long had

he been gone? *Oh my God,* I said to myself. *I could be in big trouble. I'm in a strange city in a strange country. I don't speak the language. I can't call a cab or the police because I don't know where I am. I don't even know the address. Or how to use the phone. I don't speak any German.*"

"Oh, Suzanne," Leyla said. "You must have been terrified."

I nodded. "I was scared. I felt like I was in a B movie—a dark B movie. I got up and walked over to the desk. I was looking for mail, the address. There was no mail. Only magazines—girlie magazines. I looked for an address label. None. I walked around the desk and sat in his chair. I tried the drawers. They were locked. I said to myself, *Where the hell is Bruno? How could he just walk out and abandon me? What am I going to do?*"

I continued, almost in a trance, reliving, remembering. "My stomach was rumbling. I didn't know if it was fear or hunger. I found some apples in a bowl and sat back at the desk to eat one. While I was munching, I opened one of the magazines. All the women were supersized. I'd never seen anything like that. I checked another magazine and another. And then a light exploded in my head. *Ohhh. He likes large women. He isn't turned on by me anymore because I lost weight.* I realized I might not be in danger, but I still felt helpless. I was also furious at him and at myself for being so irresponsible."

I looked at Leyla and exhaled a deep breath. "Did you ever hear of anything like that?"

Leyla put her hand on my arm. "Oh, Suzanne, that is scary. How did you get out of there?"

"Eventually, he came home and took me to the airport."

I took another deep breath and sighed. "So, dear sister. Tell me about anger. I don't get angry very often, but I was furious. I kept my mouth shut until my suitcase and I were safely out of his car at the airport terminal, and then I let him have it. I told him that if he ever showed up at any person-centered event again, I'd tell the whole world what he pulled and what a *scumbag* he is."

I looked at Leyla. "Your English is terrific. But I bet you never heard that expression before."

"Thank God you're okay. It's quite a lesson. You know, your life always looks so enticing to me . . . your freedom to have adventures without the constraints of marriage."

"Yes, but when I divorced Myles, I had nothing to lose. You do. No matter how hard I tried, Myles wasn't able to be a partner in family life like Daniel is. Myles spun a lot of seductive dreams on our honeymoon about coming to Europe every summer, renting a sailboat, raising our children to be multilingual with a broad worldview, like you've done with yours. It never happened. He didn't even come home for dinner! I love being with you and Daniel here. In fact, I must confess, I'm feeling a little 'empty nest' nostalgia for all the summers when your children were here with us on the boat. I love your family, and I love feeling a part of it."

"I'm glad you were able to share that chapter of our lives with us. Now the kids are all pursuing their studies and careers, and I don't know if any of them will even make it here this summer. I think it's been especially hard for Daniel. He seems at loose ends sometimes. I still have my precious two-hour swim every morning."

"You are a mermaid."

"Swimming is my meditation. And I love my month of September alone on the boat to write and do whatever I do with no responsibilities. But the rest of the year, I feel as if my time is not my own. I'm taking care of the family, and my therapy clients, and the young women I supervise, and the workshops I organize, and all the administrative stuff. I'm jealous of your freedom."

"Yes, I remember all the demands. That's what it was like for me at the Center. We are so alike and . . . we're also 'the road not taken' for each other. I have the freedom to 'play' without consequences, without jeopardizing a marriage. Most of the time, I don't even want a lover. I enjoy my solitude and my women friends more. I learned from my motorcycle/sailboat relationship with Ray that I really do want to be the captain of my own ship. In the beginning, I had to prove to myself that I could be attractive to men and have adventures. But I think I'm done with getting caught up in the 'story' of a week in Hawaii or a weekend in Zurich.

"I'm older than you are," I reminded us both. "Because of the laws, I couldn't even get my own credit card until after I was forty. I could only have a spouse card on Myles's account. I thought having my own credit card was enough. I could go anyplace in the world with it. I don't have to account to anyone, but I realize this thing with Bruno was irresponsible. My mantra with my daughters was, 'With freedom comes responsibility.' I guess I should start paying attention to that myself. Not only didn't anyone at home know how to find me if there was an emergency, I didn't even know myself where I was going."

I was done with my story and with the fear and the anger

it engendered. The conversation segued into Leyla's book and an intellectual/philosophical/psychological/personal discussion of women's anger. Eventually, we got hot and jumped in the water. Well, she jumped. I could jump metaphorically and psychologically, but not physically. I climbed down the ladder. The cool waters of the Mediterranean were so refreshing. However, while Leyla swam out to sea, I circled around the boat; after my Zurich folly, I wasn't going to lose my bearings again.

That evening, instead of dinner aboard the boat, the captain dropped Leyla, Daniel, and me off in the dinghy at a charming seaside restaurant. I was totally relaxed after a day of intimate conversation with Leyla, political conversation with Daniel, swimming, and reading and napping under the awning the captain and mate set up for us on the bow after lunch to protect us from the sun and afternoon heat.

After a delicious meal with small plates of salty black olives and stuffed grape leaves and eggplant, followed by fresh grilled fish, we moved to a patio for Turkish coffee. Seated around a cocktail table in comfortable cushioned rattan chairs, I assumed we were waiting for the captain or the mate to come pick us up in the dinghy. But suddenly I realized we were moving. The patio was actually a motorized raft, and someone from the restaurant was taking us back to the boat. While we sat comfortably sipping our coffees, we skimmed across the water under a star-filled, moonlit sky. It was a spiritual experience. I felt at one with the universe. I looked over at Leyla, my sister. She grinned, her eyes twinkling like the stars. She knew I'd never forget this night.

# WOMAN WITH A CAPITAL W

June 1997

A doorman in a scarlet plumed hat ushered my Italian friend Elettra and me into the palatial Hotel Negresco in Nice. Elettra had taken a time-share for a week on the French Riviera and invited me to be her guest. As we crossed the glistening white marble floor of this famous gathering place for starlets and magnates, I didn't know which way to look first. But, as we neared the center of the rotunda, we grabbed each other's arm and uttered a collective "Ah!" Our view was drawn upward to an exquisite, twinkling chandelier made of thousands and thousands of crystals, surrounded by gorgeous stained-glass windows under the hotel's famous pink dome.

When my neck started to cramp, I lowered my head, and, still standing in place, I began to circle the white colonnaded hall with my eyes. In this sumptuous building, filled with French art from centuries past, I was searching for someone in particular. Someone I wanted to meet. Someone I wanted Elettra to meet. I had read about her and asked Elettra if we could come to the Negresco for this very purpose. Then I spotted her. Slowly twirling around and around between two pairs of gilt-trimmed white columns, danced a fabulous, exuberant, banana-yellow sculpture of a woman.

I knew a little about Niki de Saint Phalle's sculpture. I'd passed by her monumental birdlike *Sun God* on my walks around the UCSD campus. But I had never encountered one of her Nanas before. She was colossal yet stood gracefully on one leg, with the other bent behind, her arms raised joyfully, all curves exaggerated, wearing a painted bathing suit with her hips in bright blue, her breasts cupped in red with decorative symbols all over them, including a charming red heart for one nipple. She was fabulous!

I exclaimed, "Oh, Elettra. Isn't she beautiful!"

My dear Italian friend rolled her eyes and replied, "How can you call her beautiful? She's so fat!"

"She's an archetypal woman," I proclaimed.

Elettra shook her head and repeated, "She's not beautiful. She's just fat."

As the sculpture slowly turned around on her revolving base, I pleaded, "Oh, Elettra, those curves are gorgeous—she's Woman with a capital *W*."

"Suzanne, I'm surprised at you. You used to be heavier, but now you're not fat at all. Obviously, you didn't think your fat was beautiful or you wouldn't have lost the weight."

"You're right about that. I didn't think my fat was beautiful." I took a deep breath, then told Elettra my secret. "On the top shelf of my closet, shoved way in back, are at least a dozen journals, each with my weight listed at the top of every entry. On page after page, I wrote messages to myself with plans to diet, strategies to give up cereal, only eat celery, fill up with water, along with little pep talks and calculations: *You can do it, Suzy. Ten pounds by the time you leave. Four pounds a week for one month and you'll be 135 by Thanksgiving.* Page after page, year after year, up and down. My weight was the subtext of my life. Though I was never more than thirty pounds overweight—usually no more than ten or fifteen—I was obsessed with my weight and dieting for years. Those journals in my closet date from all the way back when I moved to California when I was forty-six—until last year."

"So, what changed?" asked Elettra. "You're not making sense. You lost all the weight, yet now you're claiming fat is beautiful."

"It's hard for me to understand too. It wasn't until after my sixtieth birthday—only a year and a half ago—that this business of self-acceptance—of just being me—seems to have reached fruition. I was done working, I was done looking for a core primary relationship, and I was done obsessing about weight. I just went on a diet and took off the extra weight for good. Carl Rogers wrote someplace, 'The more you accept yourself, the more you change.' I guess that's what happened to me—I can dance joyfully with this Nana. She is Woman, and so am I."

I looked at Elettra. We had bonded so seamlessly when she had been my translator in my first international training gig in Rome a decade earlier. Back then she had said, "In translating your words, I was able to speak out loud so many thoughts I never had the courage to say before." But now, in this fancy hotel in France, we were not thinking alike at all. I did not take this personally; rather, I looked at it with curiosity.

"Is it a cultural thing?" I asked. "Are the blond northern

Italians like you more sylphlike, and dark-haired southerners more curvy, like Sophia Loren?"

"Oh, no," she replied, "I'm not a northerner—I dye my hair." She turned toward me. "Why don't you dye yours? You'd look younger and more attractive as a blonde."

"Actually, I was a blonde in my thirties, in the hippy era," I said. "I had long, straightened, dyed blond hair." I shrugged. "I let go of being blond by forty, but plumpness took a lot longer."

Elettra shook her head and took my arm. "Come," she said. "Let's go look for real beauty."

# ON THE EDGE

Summer 1998

At the age of sixty-two, I stood silently with my British friend Anne at the southernmost tip of Africa and looked out over the vast ocean, imagining those early explorers from Europe discovering the very tip of the continent on which we stood. I didn't know if I had my facts straight, but romantic names like Vasco da Gama and Amerigo Vespucci came to mind, all the way from sixth-grade social studies class. There is something about being on the edge, in contrast to being in the thick of things, that feels so satisfying to me, as if it's my soul's calling.

Anne and I were exploring the Cape Town area prior to participating in the Seventh International Person-Centered Approach (PCA) Forum in Johannesburg, South Africa. I had retired from CSP, but I was still interested in participating in the international forums. It felt like attending a reunion every three years. Since there was no parent organization, whoever was present at the final community meeting of each forum voted on who would host the next forum three years hence.

Individuals and organizations came to that final meeting prepared to make their pitch as to what their country would gain from a PCA event and how they could muster the resources in manpower and facilities to mount such an undertaking.

This tradition had started in Brazil in '89, when we voted for Holland in '92. In Holland we voted for Greece in '95, and in Greece, Anne and I put our weight behind the proposal from two South Africans to host the gathering in '98. Mandela had been president for a year, and we were excited to experience the new post-apartheid South Africa.

Consequently, we, the forum organizers and other participants, were all disappointed when few Black South Africans had enrolled.

On our last morning, we invited the conference center staff—all of whom were Black—into our meeting to thank them. We stood and sang the newly adopted English-language version of the South African national anthem. As we finished, Antonio dos Santos, a wiry Brazilian friend of mine, started a conga line that, under his lead, snaked into the kitchen, gathering all the kitchen workers, and then returned, collecting the rest of us South Africans and Westerners. We snaked around the center joyfully singing and dancing together. It was an extraordinary cross-cultural transcendent moment of oneness and hope.

I am so grateful that at the time of my life when I had the freedom, interest, energy, and means to travel the world, Anne came into my life to be a friend, colleague, and travel buddy. Frankly, it was more fun and more interesting for us to travel with each other than it would have been for either of us with our old married partners. I had already been single for well over a decade when we met in Brazil, and I wasn't interested in marrying again. But, once I was done with sexual adventuring, I wasn't interested in traveling alone either. Anne felt the same way.

To use her English expression, we "got on well." We both had curiosity and zest for travel, the need for downtime, and a desire to stick together. As adventurous as I may seem, I would not have been happy to go off on my own and then meet up at the end of the day as some travel companions do.

Sampling feijoada in Brazil, shepherd's pie in England, or pho in Vietnam, our dinner table conversations were always lively as we reviewed and assimilated our experiences, each through the lens of our own personality and our own culture: Anne had more reverence for the old and traditional and historic, and I leaned toward the modern and dynamic and global. I was so American; she, so British.

In nearly every restaurant in which Anne and I dined, regardless of location, I saw old married couples who did not seem engaged with each other for whatever reason: contentment, boredom, habit, resignation? We, on the other hand, single women of a certain age, were happy to have the companionship of a good female friend and enjoyed discovering the similarities and differences in our worldview. We were both explorers, excited about life and celebrating our freedom from family and career responsibilities. We were both very much enjoying living in the present.

# DEER DANCING

December 31, 1999

Step, step, hop, turn; step, step, hop, turn; step, step . . .

Around and around, we circled the drummers. Step, step, hop, turn. How many were we? More than fifty, less than one hundred? Deer dancing together to bring in the millennium. Step, step, hop, turn. *Are the drums getting louder and louder?* Step, step, hop, turn. I was in a trance. Step, step . . . the drumming reached a crescendo and stopped. No hugs and kisses or confetti flying at the magic moment of midnight. Instead, a silent procession to the sweat lodge.

My daughter Wendy wasn't allowed—she had her period. Ancient tradition. Was she impure or just more likely to faint? No matter, I was relieved. Sweat lodges pushed the limits of my claustrophobia. We peeled off from the parade and headed toward the hot tub. Clear Lake felt like a magical spot. No city lights distracted from the clear sky of Northern California. No one else joined us. Steam rose from the hot tub into the crisp winter air. As I removed my clothes, the cold air rushed against my sweaty body. Wendy was already submerged up to her neck. She reassured me, "Just sit down on the edge, Mom. You can slide right in." I leaned back and took in the vast sparkling sky, aware of what a gift it was to enter the new millennium in this sacred way together. We soaked in silence for a while, two small, interconnected dots in the cosmos.

As I entered my sixties, I began learning about Huichol shamanism the way I like best to learn—experientially. My ulterior motive was healing for Wendy, who seemed to be getting sicker and sicker with no clear diagnosis or treatment from Western medicine.

Friends of mine who were highly reputable psychologists with PhDs from UCLA were involved in a training group led by Brant Secunda, a Western-born Huichol shaman. My favorite teacher of Eastern spirituality had been Ram Dass, an East Coast Jewish ex-Harvard professor who spent years in India apprenticing himself to a Hindu teacher, who eventually sent him back to teach in the West. Brant Secunda also turned out to be a Jewish boy from the East. After graduating from high school in Teaneck, NJ, he went to Mexico on a spiritual quest and apprenticed himself for twelve years to a Huichol shaman, who transmitted his shamanic visionary and healing powers to Brant. Twelve years was considerably longer than I spent in undergraduate, graduate, and PhD programs combined, so I judged Brant as well-trained by Western standards. Wendy and I took several programs offered by his Dance of the Deer Foundation.

The first was an introductory weekend at the Glen Ivy retreat center in the mountains about an hour from my home in San Diego. Wendy, Barbara, and my friend Leyla from

Turkey attended with me. We sat on the floor in a circle of about sixty people as Brant explained some basics of the Huichol tradition, particularly the significance of the deer as the guide to the spirit world. Then Brant and members of his training group began drumming. Before we knew it, we were up deer dancing—a few steps, a hop, a turn, over and over until our minds and bodies were in an altered state of consciousness. Though the original tribal tradition included peyote, ours did not.

We sat down, and a young man entered the circle and seated himself in front of Brant for a healing. Brant drummed and chanted, then got up and did some shamanic dancing, shaking rattles and chanting in four directions. At some point, Brant told the young man to stretch out flat, then Brant crouched down and put his mouth on the patient's belly. When Brant stood up, he pulled a cloth from his pocket and spit into it, as if he had literally sucked poisonous toxin out of the prone body. He did this several times. We sat, mesmerized. After it was over, Brant invited the young man to rejoin the circle and tell us his story. He had cancer that had been getting worse until he started coming to Brant. Now, to his doctors' amazement, his cancer had been in remission for more than a year.

The next day we learned about the powers of the four directions, made god's eyes out of yarn and twigs, then climbed the mountain to bury chocolate, "planting our gifts to Mother Earth." Though Wendy was suffering from intractable back pain, she made it up the mountain and back. Several times over the next few years, she came into Huichol workshops crippled with back pain, but she participated in all the rituals anyway, including climbing hills, chanting, and lots of deer dancing. After doing the practices and having a healing session with Brant surrounded by the energy of the group, Wendy always felt better.

When my adult daughter felt better, I, as her mother, felt less powerless.

Then Brant offered an experience that grabbed me, not as a healing for Wendy, but as a challenge to *my* being—an overnight vision quest alone in the wilderness outside of Juneau, Alaska. For me, an urban and suburban girl who is *not* comfortable alone in nature, it was a formidable challenge, but one that I wanted to undertake. Wendy was game to come. When she returned from the Peace Corps, she had spent time in the Alaska wilderness with her college roommate who had become a park ranger there.

We flew to Juneau and spent two days taking day cruises to see the gorgeous glaciers. We even saw some spectacular iceberg calving. Then we took a taxi to a campground near the end of the road outside Juneau where the wilderness begins. I think there were around forty of us. Tents were scattered around the site, but I had reserved beds in the simple bunkhouse for Wendy and myself. In a large clearing with a campfire at the center, we spent several days of preparation with drumming and deer dancing, ritual, and teaching. Then we were ready to go off into the wilderness, each of us directed to create a sacred space for a vision quest, away from the sight or sound of human life. As we left the campsite, Brant and a few others began drumming, enveloping us in spirit, and keeping us safe until the last person returned to the circle the following morning. As I left, I wondered how I would know it was time to come back without wearing a watch. Wendy and I and a few other less-abled folks were offered a ride to the end of the road to give us a head start at finding our sites, ahead of those who could hike further.

I don't know if the driver said, "To the left is the ocean," or if the spirits guided me there, but after trekking through the woods in dappled light for a short while, I came into full sunlight at the edge of a beautiful cove with a pristine sandy beach. I walked across the full length of the beach, then carefully climbed the black rock cliff at the far end and set myself up on a ledge overlooking the ocean. Using stones, I delineated my sacred circle and stepped inside. I was trusting the "rock people" to support and protect me. I deliberately chose a spot away from the woods where I thought I would be safe from bears. I did get a little anxious when I heard critters of the male human-kind partying on the beach in the evening.

During the day, the view was exquisite. Occasionally I could see a large white ship in the distance along the horizon line. I replayed the blue and white beauty of the glaciers I'd seen on our day trips, but I was glad my "Alaska experience" was not on a cruise ship. I didn't know what I might learn, but I was open to the expansion of my psychological and spiritual self on this Huichol path.

I had brought walking sticks for the climbing and hiking in rituals, and I used them as stakes to hold up my tarp so I had sun protection. That in itself was a mature choice for me —to shade myself rather than spend the day basking in the sun. I was pleased with my ingenuity, and, when evening came, I was glad I was not sweaty and sunburned. I had picked a lovely spot that was not too challenging to get to. I deliberately took a simple route so I could retrace my steps across the beach without worrying about finding my way back in the morning. However, the next day when I awakened at sunrise, there was a strange new sound. The tide had come all the way in and up so high that the water was almost lapping at my toes. I couldn't descend to the beach—there was no beach.

Years later, I read that Juneau is famous for its thirty-one-foot tides. No one had told me. I had no choice but to make my way back through the brambles across the top of the cliff. My first step out of my sacred circle, with my sleeping roll on my back, I lost my balance and fell. But, after that, I got my footing. I let go of my belief about my terrible sense of direction and let myself be guided. I made it back to camp on my own and on time. I hadn't had profound visions, but I had learned that I could not only survive without food or a watch, I could also feel in tune with nature and safe outdoors. This was enough for me. "Trust the universe" was no longer a glib, new age expression; it was a personal experience. I was not just a "city girl" or a "Southern California beach girl" or even a "woman of the world," I was part of the interconnected whole universe.

Where could I go from there?

# BEST MALE FRIEND

November 2010

"Robert, look. Suzanne's here," said Helga, his wife, in a cheery falsetto voice as I entered his hospital room.

A lump caught in my throat as I looked at him, propped up in a bed in the center of the room, a ventilator mask covering his nose and mouth. For a tall man, he looked so small. The smell of the room, the beeps of machines, everything fell away as I took Robert's hand. *No!* I screamed silently. *Oh no, dear one. I know this is not what you want.* "No artificial devices. Let me go in peace," he had said so clearly. Did I imagine that he'd seemed to relax, as if he trusted that I would take care of his wishes?

I looked across at Helga, seeing the strain in her face. She had been Robert's beautiful young wife for years. I felt the strain too and asked, "How long have you been waiting for them to disconnect the ventilator?" I looked at my watch. "I think it's been almost an hour since you called me. I came right away." I don't remember waiting for her answer. I let go of Robert's hand with a gentle squeeze. "I'll go see what I can do."

"Are you Robert's nurse?" I asked the woman in blueprint scrubs alone in the office across the hall.

"Yes." She nodded. "I'm the hospice nurse. Is there anything you need?"

"I'm so glad you're a hospice nurse, then you understand. Robert never wanted artificial means to keep him alive. He's so distressed by this ventilator. What's taking so long to get it disconnected?"

"I'm so sorry—it's Sunday, and the techs seem to be busy hooking people up, and that comes first. Let me call again."

As she picked up the phone, I was transported back to the same rage I'd felt almost twenty years earlier when my father died. My fists clenched and so did my jaw. I was gripped with frustration at my inability to get Robert the relief he was pleading for. I heard my father begging, "Suzy, please take me to the bathroom. I have to go," pleading over and over again. I was back with my elderly dad in the emergency room of Scripps Encinitas, where the ambulance had brought him when his GI tract suddenly gave out in the middle of the night. He was hooked up to a urinary catheter, but he was too senile to understand that the pressure he felt in his bladder was from a catheter. My dad never asked me for anything, and there I was on his last day unable to give him what he wanted, a trip to the bathroom. I asked for a tranquilizer for him and waited and waited. Finally, in utter frustration, I marched to the hospital pharmacy and got the pill for him.

Now I wished I could disconnect Robert's ventilator myself. *Hospitals!* The hospice nurse put her hand on my shoulder. "Here comes the tech now. Why don't you wait out here?

I'll send Helga out while we get the ventilator off and I get Robert comfortable."

While Helga and I stood in the hall, Robert's daughter and son joined us. When we returned to the room, Robert seemed to be resting comfortably with the ventilator mask off his face and his eyes closed. I took his hand and whispered into his ear, "Be at peace, dear one. You can go whenever you want. You are surrounded with love." I gave his hand a little squeeze, then stepped back to begin our vigil: Helga and me on one side of the bed, his daughter and son on the other. I have no idea how much time passed. There was no dramatic last gasp. I looked up, and my eyes met those of his daughter, Mia.

"I think he's gone."

I nodded and turned to Helga. "Would you like me to get the nurse?"

"Yes," she said. Mia nodded.

I left the room and walked back across the hall. "Robert just passed," I told the nurse.

"No," she said, shaking her head. "I've been monitoring his heart. See, it's still beating."

I shook my head. "All four of us felt it."

As she stood up, she slapped her forehead with the heel of her hand. "Oh, the pacemaker! Robert's gone, but his pace-maker is still going. I have to go turn it off."

Robert would have enjoyed telling that story. I can hear his chuckle and see the twinkle in his eye.

Driving home from the hospital, my heart was full of grati-tude, love, and appreciation for my friendship with this won-derful man. It was a friendship that had begun thirteen years earlier, when I was sixty-one. I was seventy-four when he died, and he was eighty-seven. I smiled as I remembered the phone call that started it all.

September 2002

"Hi, Suzanne. This is Robert. I'm calling to find out if the statute of limitations has run out yet. Will you finally let go of being my therapist and come have lunch with me?"

"Well, okay, Robert." I chuckled. "How many years has it been since you left the therapy group? I guess the statute of limitations *has* expired."

"I don't remember exactly, but it's been a long time since you kicked me out of your group."

"Oh, Robert, you know I didn't kick you out."

After Robert got his pacemaker, I'd suggested he move to a therapy group of his peers where he could process issues about aging instead of having such a good time confronting and mentoring all the younger people in our group. When neither of us could find a seniors group for him, I fixed him up with my old CSP buddy Bruce, the founder of the La Jolla Program.

"Are you and Bruce still getting together?" I asked.

"Not so much. I'll tell you about it at lunch. I go to the gym almost every morning. I could meet you any day at noon. How about Fidel's in Solana Beach?"

Sometimes I marvel at how the universe works. I arrived at Fidel's a few minutes early. I did not order a margarita while I was waiting, though I seriously considered it, because I was quite upset.

By the time Robert arrived, I was almost teary. In he walked—tall, good-looking, salt-and-pepper hair, trim beard and mustache, wearing sweats and sneakers. He had a smile on his face, a great big shoulder to lean on, and a warm, caring heart. He reached in to give me a hug, then pulled away and asked, "Is something the matter?" In a blink, any remnant of our therapist/client relationship vanished.

*Wow,* I realized, *he picked up that I'm upset without my uttering a word.*

He sat down and leaned across the table. "What's up?"

"I just came from the eye doctor, and I guess I'm a little stunned and scared by what he had to say. I've taken eye drops for glaucoma for years, but suddenly my eye pressure is out of control. I guess deep down, I'm afraid of going blind."

Had our lunch date been scheduled a few days later, I might have been back in my "I can handle almost anything" persona, but the timing was perfect for me to allow myself to feel and share my fears, just as I had encouraged Robert to do in the group when he first got his pacemaker.

Over the next thirteen years, we became an integral part of each other's lives. He called me frequently, and we got together for an early-bird dinner once a week. When I was away too long, he sometimes called Barbara as a "Suzanne substitute." I liked feeling needed while at the same time having the freedom to go.

He met my daughters, and I met his daughter and her family. After his granddaughter was born, it warmed my heart to watch him move into the role of family patriarch, making up for the dysfunctional family he had as a child.

When I review all the men with whom I've had ongoing

relationships in my adult life, Robert is number one. He was so like my father. Both were dynamic, totally self-made, self-educated sons of Jewish immigrants who transcended hard, challenging New York childhoods to become American success stories. They also both had a passion for social justice. They would have liked each other. Where they differed was that Robert had a deep empathic understanding of people that my father did not have. Consequently, Robert understood and appreciated me in all the ways my father never did. What a gift that was.

And it was mutual. I understood Robert's New York Jewish roots in ways his beautiful, bright, foreign-born, non-Jewish wife could not. Over the last decade of his life, she came to see and appreciate me as his best friend. Helga knew I was not a threat to their marriage. She would say, "After dinner with you, he comes home with more understanding of me." Eventually, when he could no longer drive, she would drop him off at a favorite Persian restaurant in Del Mar, and I would bring him home so she could get a little time off to go to a movie.

I knew all about his amazing life by then. My heart swelled when he showed me his inventions, awards, photos, and other memorabilia. The understanding and appreciation we gave each other was precious.

I have mutual understanding, acceptance, and support in all my close relationships, and except for Robert, they have all been with women. Sexual or not, there is a special quality of loving, understanding friendship with someone of the opposite gender, at least for me as a heterosexual. Some people have this in their marriages. Many men say, "My wife is my best friend. I can talk to her in ways I can't with men." Rarely do I hear a woman say, "My husband is my best friend," especially a woman of my generation. Mostly women say, "My women friends 'get' me in ways my husband just doesn't." For me, it was special to be known and appreciated in the ways Robert valued me.

For me, this was ideal. We had a mutual respect, admiration, appreciation, and love without the responsibility of caretaking. I was willing and able to physically take care of myself and not interested in looking after a partner. A daily phone call and weekly get-together were sufficient, without all the compromises and conflicts of daily life and responsibility. Our friendship added a precious intimacy to my life while still leaving me free to be the captain of my own ship on the shifting seas of my sixties.

# CHANGING OF THE GUARD

"Oh, Suzy, just look at the green. Isn't it beautiful!" It was the year 2000, and my ninety-five-year-old mother and I were sitting in the den of her condo in Solana Beach. I sat on the beige easy chair with my back to the window and sliding glass door, so she could sit on the couch and look out at the golf course. "Your father always wanted water, never green. Our East River view was interesting with all that boat traffic and the UN and the bridge, but once we moved to Longboat Key, the Gulf view was so boring. I didn't really care how well I played; I just loved walking the course."

*What?* I said to myself. *Ah, she's switched tracks. Gulf to golf. Just let her go.* I'd learned that if I corrected her by saying, "Mom, you were talking about Florida with Dad. Then you switched to when you learned to play golf when you were eighteen, before you met Dad," she would get upset and say, "Oh, Suzy, what's happening to me? I'm losing my mind."

I didn't want to make her feel bad about something she couldn't control, so I just listened to the eight-track player that was her ninety-five-year-old mind and tried to be with her on whatever track she skipped to. I knew all her stories, so it was kind of fun. Eight-track is an exaggeration. She never had more than four story lines going at once. She wasn't loopy all the time, but she sure did like to reminisce.

Mom continued, "Once I got those golf clubs, I took the subway up to the Bronx every Saturday that I could. Did I ever tell you how I got those clubs?"

She had, a million times, but I let her tell me again. My mother was back being eighteen.

"I was in my first job out of high school. My father was still working, so I was taking classes at Columbia University at night. In high school, I worked for Mr. Linkler, the principal, and he taught me how to keep the books. When I graduated, I got a job as a bookkeeper in a men's clothing firm. At Christmastime, one of the salesmen, who was always trying to butter me up so I'd get his orders processed faster, sidled up to my desk and asked me, "What do you want for Christmas, Miss Cohen?" So I answered, "Golf clubs."

"Mom, how did a New York City daughter of simple immigrant parents even know about golf clubs and golf courses?"

"Honey, I'm not sure. I don't remember. Maybe it was my Aunt Lena. I adored her. She was more Americanized, not like my mother who only spoke Yiddish. I learned a lot from Aunt Lena."

"Did your Aunt Lena play golf?" I asked with my eyebrows raised.

"Oh no. It must have been someone I went out with. You know that all the guys I went out with were more polished than your father. Your father and I were just friends for a long time before I married him. He used to tell me about his dates and make fun of me for being 'hoity-toity.'"

I laughed. "You always were more proper than Dad, but you married him anyway."

"Well, once my father got sick and I had to support my parents, I didn't want to have to be asking one of those rich guys for money. I realized your father would understand my need to work because he had to support his mother and sister."

She was off on a track about falling in love with my dad when Isabella, her caretaker, came into the den, saying, "Sorry to interrupt, but it's eye drop time." I sat back and let Isabella take over. I appreciated her attentive caregiving and the close relationship she and my mom had developed.

With their sweet chatter as background, I went back in my mind through that awful chapter eight years earlier, just before Isabella became part of our family. It was June 1991, and my parents had arrived in San Diego for what had become their annual summer escape from the Florida heat and humidity. I was shocked at the progression of my father's senility and the toll it was taking on my mother. He was totally confused and asked my mother over and over and over again, "Where am I?" and "When's dinner?"

I insisted they stay near me in San Diego permanently. My mother agreed—she couldn't get back on an airplane with my dad. She would not consider putting him into an assisted living facility because he had been in an orphanage for a few years as a young child after his father died—we both felt awful about that. I wondered if his senile obsessive asking, "When is dinner?" came from standing in line with a tin cup in the orphanage. I rented a two-bedroom furnished apartment for them and hired nurse's aides to help with my dad at home while we sold their Florida apartment and found them an unfurnished condo on the golf course in Solana Beach. When their furniture arrived from Florida, my mother gave me three days to get everything unpacked, beds made with bedspreads on, paintings hung, and the kitchen all in order. She had her heart set on moving in on December 29—their sixty-third wedding anniversary. Her hope was that seeing all their familiar furniture would jog my father out of his senility. It was magical thinking, but it was sweet.

The doorbell rang at five o'clock on the 29th. It was the nurse's aide delivering my father as scheduled from the furnished apartment where my parents had been living. I stayed back and let my mother open the door. "Happy anniversary, darling," she said. "Come in. You're home. Come see."

My father looked at her blankly and asked, "Where's the bathroom? I gotta go." That was all. It was heartbreaking. Less than two weeks later, he was rushed to the hospital and died peacefully later that day. He was almost ninety-two.

My mother wanted a simple traditional Reform Jewish funeral service. El Camino Memorial Park was set in lush rolling green grounds in nearby Sorrento Valley. I knew she'd like the green. It was much prettier than driving out from Manhattan through the ugly commercial warehouse streets of Long Island City to the overcrowded New York Jewish cemeteries. But to me, El Camino had no soul. They put a Jewish star or a cross on the podium depending on the religion of the deceased. The room they gave us was too big for our small family. Barbara was the only one of my friends who knew my dad. If we'd been in New York, we would have needed a room large enough to accommodate representatives from the advertising industry and the charities where my dad had been such a leader until his retirement. But we were far away from his roots and his American success story.

We hired a rabbi who led the service, including the traditional Kaddish prayer for the dead. I gave a eulogy. I cherished my dad and got my maverick ways from him. Wendy spoke too. She adored her grandfather, and it was mutual. She honed her debating skills on him starting at age six when she put her hands on her hips and sputtered, "But Grandpa, you were just arguing the opposite. You can't do that. You can't switch sides." He'd grinned from ear to ear and replied, "That's called playing devil's advocate, honey." Oh, the smile from him and the frown from her. She became an assistant district attorney.

Within a week of my dad's passing, Isabella entered our lives. I replayed that scene in my head—my mother was sitting on the couch in the den in exactly the same position she was in now, facing out to the green golf course. I answered the doorbell and brought Isabella into the room. Mom patted the couch and invited Isabella to sit with her. I sat across from them in the easy chair; I let my mother ask all the questions. I didn't know if it was her old human resource interviewing skills or simply that she was always interested in people and their stories, but sitting there, at age eighty-seven, her life force was back, and she hadn't lost her touch. It was almost love at first sight between my mother and Isabella and therefore between Isabella and me. I knew the match was made when Isabella explained that she'd come from Guatemala to earn money to support her mother and kids when her husband was murdered while making a weekly bank deposit for his business. Of course, my mom responded to Isabella's hardship and resilience. She herself had supported her parents and, eventually, her older sisters too.

Mom adopted Isabella's family, and they adopted her. Every year for Christmas she brought Isabella's children, and sometimes her mother and nephew, from Guatemala to San Diego for a visit. She and Isabella had a wonderful loving chapter together. Not only did my mom have green outside of her every window, Isabella took her on drives almost daily around Rancho Santa Fe and other lush spots. The green was an intravenous boost to her life force.

I came out of my reverie and suddenly realized Isabella had been standing there listening to my mother the whole time I'd been reminiscing. I finally said, "Isabella, why are you standing? Come sit down with us."

"Actually, I'm standing because I was going to ask how long you're staying. If you're planning to be here awhile with your mom, I was going to go to the store."

I'll never forget what happened next. After Isabella left for her errand, neither my mother nor I had other places to be or things to do. As we sat talking, she suddenly looked at me in a kind of stunned realization and said, "You know, Suzy —you really are a terrific woman."

I smiled, took it in, and replied, "I stand on your shoulders, Mom."

Driving home that day, I was all smiles inside. I was sixty-four; this whole last chapter with my mom so close was such a gift. My childhood yearning for relaxed connection and acceptance from her was fulfilled. I always knew she loved me, but when I was growing up, she was usually tense, with too many responsibilities to be able to just sit and talk. Even years later when I visited my parents in Florida, my mother was always busy with "things to do." But with both of us now retired, I was able to appreciate what a positive role model she had been. We were both women who'd carved out lives on our own terms, creating meaningful careers when that wasn't the norm for either of our generations, though it had been infinitely less acceptable in her time. What I had done beyond her was leave my marriage and create a fulfilling, happy life for myself as a single woman, first in California and then out in the rest of the world. I think my mom realized in that moment just how happy and fulfilled I was—and I, in turn, realized how much I owed to her.

My mother died at peace, at home, a month before her ninety-sixth birthday. I had called my brother Mal in New York and insisted, "If you want to see Mom alive, you must come THIS weekend. No more delays." She had been missing him. She was ready to go, but she needed to see her beloved son one more time. She was waiting. He and my sister-in-law Harriette got on an airplane and arrived from New York on Friday night. Less than twenty-four hours later, our mom passed.

I knew I did not want to go back to El Camino Memorial Park. Instead of a traditional service, we had a memorial celebration with the family and my friends who by then all knew my incredible mom. We made a big circle in my living room. I arranged for a rabbi to say Kaddish, then we sat around and told Mima stories for hours. "Did Mima ever tell you about the night she danced on a table in a speakeasy when she was a flapper?" I asked. My daughters were shocked. They all told stories of "the look" when they didn't meet her standards of proper behavior. My friends Barbara and Liv planted flowers to spruce up the patio and took care of all the good Jewish deli food including corned beef and pastrami, my mother's favorites, which my daughters and I would never touch.

Before they returned to their own lives, Wendy, Donna, and Sharrin followed me down the stairs of my condo and through the garage. We crossed the driveway, the back lawn, and the dry creek bed through which water gushes once a year in February. When we reached the stately palm that dominates the view from my living room and upstairs bed-room, we stopped and stood together in the vibrant, lush green, wild nasturtium bed sprinkled with bright yellow and orange blossoms. I announced, "This is where I want to scatter Mima's ashes." I opened the cardboard box I was carrying and took a deep breath. Then I reached in, took a handful, and let it go in a gentle caress. "Rest in peace, dear Mother, you will always be with me. You were an extraordinary woman and an incredible example. Thank you for everything." Tears were flowing down my cheeks as I passed the box on to my daughters. One after another, Wendy, Donna, and Sharrin said goodbye to their precious Mima. When the box was empty, our hearts were full. We said one final mourner's Kaddish.

I used to have fantasies of leaving instructions for my daughters to scatter my ashes somewhere exotic, like the Great Barrier Reef, so they would have an excuse to take a big trip together. But now I think they'd be better off with the money if there is any left. I'd be perfectly content resting forever with my mom in that special nook in my green backyard, between the stately palms, in the bed of wild nasturtiums that bloom in the spring. But do I care? I don't tell my daughters what to do. I'm not going to start now.

Three months after my mother died, my grandson Julian was born. I was sixty-five. Of all the mainstream mother/daughter things Donna and I share, like shopping and pedicures and the *Outlander* series, the one I am most grateful for is that she made me a grandmother. I raised my daughters to be independent women, and sometimes I wondered if the consequence would be that grandmothering was not in the cards for me. Barbara had been generously sharing her grandchildren with me for several years, but all that sweet joy did not prepare me for the bliss I felt when my son-in-law Jeremy put Julian into my arms. The magic of that experience is indescribable. My heart turned to goo.

In the beginning, they lived only an hour away. But when they moved to Redlands, the two-hour ride each way was more than I could sit through in one day, so I drove every other weekend and stayed overnight on their living room couch. I loved being there for bath time and bedtime and Julian waking up in the morning. I loved pushing him in his swing and taking him for walks. I was happy to babysit so that Donna and Jeremy could go out and I could have my grandson alone. Julian taught me every train in Thomas the Tank Engine's yard. When Kai was born three years later, I stayed with Julian. I'll never forget that sweet moment when they brought Kai home and placed him in his big brother's arms. I waited my turn.

One night when Julian was four, after we'd done the whole bathroom and toothbrushing routine, he climbed into bed and moved over to make room for me. I knew he was expecting *Hop on Pop*—we'd been reading it every night, and we both knew it by heart.

"Hey, Julian," I suggested, "I see *The Cat in the Hat* in your bookcase—that's another Dr. Seuss book. How about reading that?" I didn't know that *The Cat in the Hat* was a much longer, more complex book than *Hop on Pop*. I sat down on the bed, and we wiggled ourselves into the reading position—leaning back against the headboard, Julian under the covers, me with my legs stretched out on top of his quilt. He opened the book, and I suggested, "Why don't you start?" To our utter amazement, Julian started reading and just kept on going and going, page after page—not just the three-letter words. Occasionally I helped him out with a tricky word, but then he got it right for all the other similar words. His voice got tired, but he kept going until he reached the end. I exclaimed, "Julian, you read that whole book! You know how to read! You're going to have so much fun reading books."

He gave me a big smile, but his eyes were already at half-mast. I said, "I bet you're tired. That was a big book." His head was already on the pillow. I gave him a kiss, and he mumbled something about the night-light. I turned it on, turned out the ceiling light, and left the room.

I don't think he knew until then that he could read; I certainly didn't know. Donna didn't believe me when I told her. She insisted, "He's just memorized it, like *Hop on Pop*." I shook my head. "No. He's reading."

She looked at me, exasperated. "Mah-ahm, his teacher would have said something if he had started reading."

"You'll see," I continued. "Why don't you let him read to you in the morning and let him bring that book to school tomorrow to read to his teacher too."

I didn't get to have that kind of experience with Kai because Donna, Jeremy, and the boys moved to the Midwest where Jeremy got a tenure-track teaching position. Anyway, Kai taught himself to read when he was three!

For the rest of my sixties and seventies, they came every summer. We converted my studio into an office for Donna's online job during the day and a bedroom for the boys to sleep on blow-up mattresses at night. It was pretty wonderful for all of us. One year on our beach walks, Kai attempted to teach me every single one of Harry Potter's magic spells. After that, it was the seemingly endless array of creatures in the Pokemon world and all their powers and characteristics.

When I bought my condo a few months after my dad died in 1992, I did not envision that it would become a summer and Christmas vacation home for my family. Back then, my daughters and I were all unmarried and leading independent lives, all on the West Coast but stretched from San Diego to Seattle. I was very grateful that Nana's house became the boys' second home until they became teenagers with lives of their own.

———

Another sweet piece of my generational family tapestry was the interweaving of my family and Barbara's over the almost forty years after we left the school and the East Coast. Barbara's son Steven and his family reconnected with my daughter Donna and her family when they were all living near each other in Southern California. Steven and Jeremy were both working on their dissertations and on track to becoming college professors. Back when Donna was four and Steven five, Barbara had dropped them off at a classmate's birthday party one Saturday afternoon. When I rang the doorbell two hours later to pick them up, the Mom explained that Donna had complained of a tummy ache at the beginning of the party, and Steven had volunteered to stay inside and keep her company while the rest of the children played wildly outside in the backyard. He hadn't even abandoned her for cake and ice cream. I walked into the living room and there they were, sitting on the living room couch with Steven's arm around Donna's shoulders.

And there we were, Steven and Donna and the rest of us, forty years later in my California condo with Kai, age four, and Steven's younger daughter, Sara, age five, sitting together in my modern red rocking chair with Kai reading to Sara. Throughout their childhoods, Kai and Sara read and played math games and computer games together whenever we got together, winter and summer. For a while, Barbara got to share this sweet generational repeat of special friendship between our children and grandchildren. But then, when I was sixty-eight and Barbara was turning seventy, she moved to Ashland, Oregon, where her oldest child, Joanne, and her husband and their three young children had settled. Steven and his family continued to come for Thanksgivings, Passovers, and the summer and Christmas visits with Donna and her family. Sometimes Barbara came too, and we got to enjoy being nanas together.

———

When I was raising my children, I saw to it that my parents and in-laws were an integral part of my daughters' lives. One or both sets of grandparents were at our house on Sundays for their granddaughters' performances in the living room, sometimes followed by dinner at the China Quarter in Tenafly. We also took the girls into the city for lots of cultural outings alone with their grandparents. They were adored and it was mutual.

My life with my grandsons had a different but equally wonderful structure because they came to spend summers and Chanukah/Christmas with me. We had a lot of time when they were young to enjoy each other, which has meant the world to me.

All in all, over the years, when I thought of my family and extended family—my daughters and their spouses, my grandsons, my brother and sister-in-law and their three children and their families, and Barbara, her children, and their families, I felt embraced. I knew I was in their hearts, as they were in mine, even though we weren't always in regular contact.

And when I thought about the changing of the guard, with my parents dying, and my grandsons growing from babies in my arms to six-foot-tall young men, I realized the circle of life was moving me toward my final turn. I truthfully couldn't imagine being any place but San Diego. My condo held a lot of loving memories, and when I pondered the inevitable, I imagined my family and extended family congregating there with my friends to tell their stories of me, a woman who . . . I knew their stories would be different from mine, but I hoped they would be filled with love and laughter, along with some raised eyebrows. Then again, I had to entertain it was possible nothing about my life would surprise my daughters anymore. I wondered, without a medical diagnosis to give you a boot in the butt, did anyone really seriously contemplate their demise?

# STRETCHING MYSELF

Fall 2011

In my two-thousand-square-foot, multi-level condo, I found only one spot in which I could do my stretching exercises— only one spot in the whole place with carpet on the floor and no furniture next to the wall. So that was my spot. Every morning, in my bedroom, I challenged myself to get down on the floor without leaning on the bed to support my descent. It wasn't an easy process: First, I leaned forward, my knees bent until my fingertips touched the floor. Then I walked my hands out, straightening my elbows and knees until the magic moment when I felt safe to swing my butt onto the floor.

Once seated, I backed up, scooting my butt as close to the wall as I could get. Then I swiveled ninety degrees, lay back with my legs on the wall, and opened them as wide as I could. *Okay, breathe. Breathe into the stretch.* As I opened my eyes and looked up the wall, staring down at me were these large, wonderful portraits of my parents—painted by me! Doing these exercises stretched my body; looking at my parents stretched my heart. Knowing I was the conduit through which the souls of these two amazing people were captured on canvas stretched my consciousness to embrace the muse who had waited patiently my whole life for me to open to her.

I would sometimes ask myself, *How did this happen—I, a brain and heart person with no artistic ability, created these paintings?* Oh, I was creative alright. I created a school, and teacher training programs, and lots of other meaningful learning experiences for people all over the world. But I was never artistically creative.

When I turned sixty, I made the decision to retire from CSP, therapy, and consulting, and begin exploring artistic expression. I signed up for sculpture classes at the Athenaeum in La Jolla and at San Dieguito Adult School. I loved the feeling of shaping the clay. Eventually, I was pleased with my final products. My last three nudes were far superior to my earlier attempts. One of these figures still sits on my coffee table today, another on a stand in my front room (my former therapy office), and the third is propped sideways on my outdoor fountain so her missing leg doesn't show.

However, pleased as I was with my figures, I decided after a year or two I didn't want to "major in" sculpture before trying other art media. While I loved shaping things, I also loved color, so I signed up for oil painting classes at MiraCosta College. It was in one of those classes that my parents' portraits emerged.

We were given an assignment to create a diptych. I chose my favorite photo of each of my parents: my mom at Donna's wedding wearing her jaunty straw hat at age ninety-one; my dad in his fifties, sitting in his office with his sleeves rolled up, thinking, visioning. I got my visionary ability from him. The painting teacher instructed us to draw graph lines over an enlarged photo, then paint, section by section. It seemed mechanical, but it worked. As I lie stretching on the floor, day after day, year after year, looking up at my parents, I am astounded at how well I captured the spirit, the essence, of each of them. My medium was water-based oil paint, but I was so timid and so sparing in the use of paint that they actually look more like watercolors than oils.

After that experience, I took a series of oil-painting classes with live models; those oils hang in my garage. I thought they were quite lovely, but they were more the teacher than me, so I decided not to hang them in the house. I enjoy them in my garage to this day. I tried plein air landscape painting too, and none of those canvasses even made it into the garage, though a water lily pond I copied from a photo hangs in Donna's house.

Eventually, I felt a yearning to express something from inside without reference to external reality, so I switched to collage and abstract acrylic painting. My abstract paintings and collages were amateurish, but they were entirely mine. I hung them all over my condo; to this day, I enjoy looking at my work and still have a kind of childlike amazement that they came out of me.

What I learned on this journey was that my artist muse did appear, but not with a full deck. When I did art, I took great pleasure in expressing myself, but I did not have the same degree of talent I had for creating institutions and experiences that facilitated others' development. That was okay. I had new empathy for those who struggle to do the things I do easily. The humbling yet fulfilling experience of trying to express myself artistically led me, in my sixties, to a deeper level of self-acceptance. I realized "comparative mind" might continue to pop up now and then until the day I die, but more and more I find myself enjoying "just" being me.

# PART IV

———

## My 70s
### BEING

# JUMPING IN

September 2006

"All you have to do is jump, Mom. See, like everybody else is doing, right over the side of the boat. I'll go first, and then you follow me. You can close your eyes if you want to. I'll be there in the water waiting for you, and I'll hold your hand."

I looked around in every direction; all I could see was the ocean. No shore, no islands, no other boats, just deep, blue, rippling ocean.

Wendy jumped in. Trusting her, I closed my eyes and jumped too. I rose to the choppy surface, gasped for a breath, opened my eyes, and, to my great relief, there she was. She helped me adjust my mask and snorkel, then took me by the hand to lead me in and around beautiful reefs, pointing out extraordinary underwater wonders. We were offshore, near the islands of Fiji. Sometimes the ocean was rough, but we persevered. Wendy never let go of my hand. What an experience! What a gift! It was so tender, sweet, and generous of her to guide me through the amazing world she so adored below the surface of the sea. I had metaphorically leaped numerous times in my life. But at seventy, I was challenging myself to do it physically. All those summers on the Navarros' boat in the south of Turkey, I always climbed down the ladder, never having the courage to jump. What a way to celebrate turning seventy.

I haven't written much about my daughters in this memoir. That's been a conscious choice—to respect their privacy and tell my story rather than theirs. However, when I reflect on my life, what means the most to me are my relationships with Wendy, Donna, and Sharrin. They were born into a typical New York Jewish, middle-class family, but our family became atypical for women of my generation. When I became involved in Montessori education, I not only stopped being a stay-at-home mom—almost unheard of in my peer group—I also moved further and further into uncharted waters as I created a school and tried to manifest, both at the school and at home, my belief in promoting each child's unique individuality and self-responsibility.

For the most part, I let my daughters fly with support and not much resistance from me. They knew they could come to me if they wanted to. Although their grandparents were strong transmitters of traditional upper-middle-class Jewish values, I was a role model of breaking free and following your own path. I am so proud of the women they each became.

During my fifties and sixties, while I was "gallivanting" (a word my mother used) around the world with my European friends, my daughters were forging their own ways into adulthood through graduate schools, travels, jobs, and relationships. By the time they were in their forties, I wanted to "gallivant" with them too. I invited the three of them on a trip to Australia to celebrate my seventieth birthday. They responded to my invitation in typical fashion.

Donna: "Sounds great, Mom, but I can't come. Unlike my sisters, I have responsibilities. The boys are too little."

Sharrin: "Sounds great, Mom. I had such a good time with you in Bali, but as I've watched you go off with your European friends, I've wondered if we'd ever travel together again. I'd love to go with you, and I'll see how much time I can work out to be away. How long will the trip be?"

Wendy: "Great idea, Mom. When I was there on my Asia trip after law school, I mostly spent time around Sydney. I'd love to see more of that fabulous country. You know, if we're going all that way, we should really go up to Kakadu National Park in the Top End and down south to Tasmania. Oh, it's going to be fun to help you plan! Gee, if Sharrin is going, maybe we should both get recertified for scuba diving. How would you feel about that? Could we go to the Great Barrier Reef?"

It was fun to plan. Wendy and I began researching in travel guides. Sharrin was happy to go along with whatever we chose. Because we wanted to do so much, I hired a travel agent to put it all together efficiently with reservations and transportation. Wendy, Sharrin, and I spent a whole hassle-free month in Australia, enjoying each other's company immensely as well as the culture and sights up and down the east coast. On the first day, we discovered flat whites—the Aussie version of lattes. We all agreed barramundi was our favorite Australian fish, only to learn when we returned that it was actually sea bass at home. Sharrin left us in Melbourne to return to work while Wendy and I went on to Tasmania, Fiji, and New Zealand. There were so many marvelous moments, and I was thrilled to experience them with my daughters after so many years of us each primarily "doing our own thing."

The most mystical moment occurred on Kangaroo Island—a ferry ride from the coast at Adelaide. A local guide drove us down a dirt road, parked the van, and unlocked an iron gate. Wendy, Sharrin, and I followed him in silence to the edge of a private savannah, then stood and watched. There, in the stillness as the sun set, first five, then ten, then fifty, then hundreds of kangaroos emerged from the surrounding trees to romp and feed on the open plain. We watched, transfixed until it was too dark to see.

The most charming moment happened when Wendy and I were having coffee at an outdoor café in a small village in New Zealand. Sitting up in an open carriage near us was the most adorable baby with fat, cherubic cheeks. A character came walking down the street in a checkered shirt, red suspenders, droopy pants, straggly gray beard, and a funny stovepipe hat. As he passed, we raised an eyebrow at each other when we saw he was leading a llama on a leash. When he stopped to chat with someone at the café, the llama leaned in and gave that baby a great big kiss. And what did she do? She leaned right in and kissed him back.

The most stupefying moment was on our first night in Tasmania. After dinner, Wendy and I were walking back to our cabin in the dark on a wooded path. Dinner had been a little challenging because Wendy had severe laryngitis and, after sunset, it was too dark for me to read her written responses. The walk back also presented challenges; after a couple of glasses of wine, I was looking down as I walked, concentrating on following my flashlight trail when, suddenly, a wallaby jumped in front of me, put his forelegs on my shoulders, and gave me a great big hug. I just stood there paralyzed, as voiceless as Wendy.

But the most surprising, magical story of all is how Wendy met her future husband, David, in Sydney the first week of our trip. Wendy and Sharrin attended a dinner gathering at a restaurant arranged by a woman Wendy had met in a hotel elevator in Chicago a month before we left. Wendy had asked, "Is that an Aussie accent I hear?" and the woman had replied, "Yes, I'm from Sydney." Instead of getting off at her floor, Wendy had ridden down to the lobby with this woman and said, "Oh, I'm going to be in Sydney next month with my mother and sister." After they chatted a bit, the woman said, "Here's my card. Call me when you're in town. I'll arrange a get-together for dinner with some of my friends." Wendy was reluctant to even call the woman because "it's your birthday trip, Mom," but I insisted. Wendy and Sharrin wanted me to go with them, but I was content with a glass or two of Australian white wine and smoked salmon canapés in the hotel rooftop lounge.

Wendy and David met that night at the dinner. The next day, they met alone for coffee at a museum café while Sharrin and I explored the fascinating aboriginal art. That first week in Sydney, it was too rainy and windy for us to enjoy the harbor life, so I decided to book an extra week in Sydney when we returned from New Zealand at the end of our trip. That add-on gave Wendy and David enough time together to spark a romance. The rest is history. David emigrated and became an American citizen. They are married and live in the Bay

Area. I love this story! Wendy was forty-six when they met. If she hadn't asked, "Is that an Aussie accent I hear?" in that Midwest elevator...

I love the partners each of my daughters chose, and I was happy I could give each of them the wedding they wanted, each as unique as they are: Donna and Jeremy in a beautiful Victorian garden in Orange, California, in 1997; Wendy and David at a lovely hotel in Las Vegas in 2007; and Sharrin and Pat, when gay marriage became legal in 2012, on a spectacular ocean cove just south of San Francisco. My daughters were all adult women when they married, not the young ingenue I'd been at twenty-two, auditioning for the role of grown-up.

# ART AND SOUL

May 2008

Intuitive Painting

Barbara and I entered a large white studio and were immediately drawn to a long table in the middle covered with paintbrushes, plastic trays, and an array of luscious paints—maybe thirty colors. Twenty cardboard carrels filled the rest of the room. "I'm so glad you're here," I said. "This is our first art adventure together."

"We've had lots of other adventures," she said, smiling. "But I was busy working when you started taking all those art classes. I love being retired now too. I can't wait to get into those paints!"

We had signed up for a two-day intuitive painting workshop at Liberty Station, an arts community in the former barracks of the Naval Training Center in the Point Loma area of San Diego.

The old adage "When the student is ready, the teacher will appear," was about to manifest for me once again, as it had twice before in my life: Nancy Rambusch had appeared in my twenties, first in a book (*Learning How to Learn*) and then in person to teach me about early childhood education, and Carl Rogers had appeared in books (*On Becoming A Person, Freedom to Learn, On Encounter Groups*) in my thirties and forties and then in person to teach me about learning to trust yourself and helping others to do the same. In my sixties I explored art making of all sorts: sculpture, oil painting, and then acrylics —landscape, portrait, still life, abstract, collage. It was all challenging and fun and I enjoy having some of my creations, amateur as they may be, scattered about my condo. But after I turned seventy, I reached a place of disquietude in my art making. At seventy-two, I was yearning to bring something forth from the inside out, rather than trying to master techniques and explore art media from the outside in. What I didn't quite know I was looking for was an expressive exploration at the intersection of creativity and spirituality, an experience that might bring together the many aspects of self I had been developing for three decades.

Laura Hansen, an expressive arts teacher, became my guide on that journey. Unlike my introduction to my previous two mentors, I met Laura in person and through her teaching, not from a book. She had organized an intuitive painting workshop for her mentor from San Francisco, but it was Laura, rather than her teacher, to whom I was drawn.

Twenty of us sat in a circle to introduce ourselves, then we each took a large sheet of paper and tacked it up in what would be our private carrel for the weekend. We proceeded to the paint table and were directed to choose a brush and the colors we were most drawn to. With relish, I poured my colors onto the plastic tray I would be using as my palette.

We reassembled in front of our carrels, and Chris, Laura's mentor, began to talk about the intuitive painting process. She emphasized, "What matters is what is going on inside of you and not what is happening on the page in front of you. The focus of the workshop is on the practice of valuing process over product. Although we are using painting, a visual medium, to express ourselves, we will not be focusing on the visual result of our efforts."

Laura then explained, "We are trying to learn to pay attention to what we are feeling and sensing AS we paint, not what we feel because of what the painting looks like. We are trying to learn to value creativity not for the product it produces but as a practice of having a conversation with ourselves, seeing ourselves more clearly, and understanding ourselves more deeply." She finished by saying, "In this way of doing art, it doesn't really matter what the painting looks like. By the end of the weekend, you will love some of your paintings and hate others. But what you can be guaranteed to get from each of your paintings is an opportunity to know yourself and feel deeply alive by directly experiencing what is going on inside you and expressing it creatively."

I resonated deeply with this teaching and said to myself, *This is just what I've been longing for.* I knew right away I was in the right place.

Chris encouraged us: "Simply let your impulses and your brushes lead you."

We began.

I made several paintings that first day. Each time I thought I was finished, I raised my hand, and Laura came over to guide me further with simple questions.

"If you were going to add another color, what would it be?" "Where would you put another color?" "What are three things you *could* add to your painting?" "Do any of those ideas have any 'juice' for you?"

By "juice" I guessed she meant energy, but I shrugged my shoulders, not knowing the right answer. Laura explained, "The energy might be excitement, a subtle quickening, or it might be a sense of aversion, resistance, or fear." When I felt neutral and there was no further impulse or energy for a painting, it was finished, and I could sign it and start another one. But if there was any "juice" in any of the ideas, then her instruction was to follow the energy and keep painting. Sometimes after doing one thing the painting would be finished, but other times doing that one thing would open up the painting (and me) in a whole new direction. I was painting from the inside out, letting the brush and the paint lead the way. All kinds of creative stuff was happening that I wasn't *making* happen. By the end of the weekend, as Laura had promised, I felt deeply enlivened.

Barbara and I laid our precious artwork in the trunk of my car and drove home, bubbling over. "That was so much fun," she said. "I can't wait to get back to the house to look at all my paintings again."

"Me too. Do you remember the eight-year-old's painting we put on the cover of the Children's Center brochure a long time ago? That's how I feel right now—like a happy child. I could start another painting with a bright yellow childlike sun."

"Funny thing—the painting I spent the most time on was a childlike house; I felt like I was in kindergarten. I'd love to show it to you if you promise not to say anything."

"I would love to see it and share mine too. Let's do 'show-and-tell' when we get home. We got the message, 'No artistic judgment.'"

"Here we go again. Another way to share how we felt and what got triggered in the process, not how it looks."

"Yeah, we were both raised on 'how it looks.' And all the painting and sculpture classes I've taken before emphasized the way it looks. I like this shift."

When Laura followed by offering a series of intuitive painting classes at her home studio, I signed up. I wanted more of the inner journey this kind of inside-out creativity was taking me on. Laura and her style of teaching expressive arts helped me discover the "visual vocabulary" of my soul, and she has been my guide, facilitator, and dear friend ever since.

For two months, we met weekly in her lush, tropical garden that was surrounded by the house on two sides and enclosed by trees and plants on the other sides, creating a sanctuary of total privacy. The sounds of birds chirping and water trickling into a pool completed the tranquil atmosphere. Cardboard carrels were scattered about the grounds, each with a stool and folding TV table. A large table filled with brushes and delicious colored paints in transparent plastic bottles beckoned seductively in the middle of the patio. Steps led up to other areas of the garden in which more cardboard carrels had been placed, but I chose one for myself close to the paints with a clear view of a towering stone Buddha serenely standing in the emerald-green foliage closest to the house.

Laura invited us to join her around the paint table as she

laid the ground rules: "No talking, and no comments on each other's work. No 'What's that?' queries or 'That's beautiful' judgments.

"One of the things we're trying to work with here is radically shifting our relationship to the judging mind," she explained. "Most of the time, we pay the most attention to the part of us that evaluates and assesses something based on our internal compass of 'good' and 'bad'—it's the part of our mind we think has the most value. But we don't realize that having an instant opinion about something puts it immediately in a box and doesn't allow us to simply *be with* what it is *for itself*. We're not going to completely get rid of our opinions, but we can observe what we think or feel about a painting (including our own) and simply not say what we are thinking. It's a way of practicing mindfulness. The goal is to get out of the thinking, judging mind and be present, creating in the moment, listening to our impulses, our intuitions."

*Okay,* I said to myself. *These are two big challenges for me. When I'm doing artwork, I'm quick to judge my work negatively, and I'm quick to get paralyzed with feelings of ineptitude instead of listening to my intuition.* I was excited. I had much to learn from this process.

Finally, Laura repeated the fundamental instructions we had been given in the weekend workshop: "Go for process, not product. Just let your brush lead you. Pick a color. Pick a brush. Make a mark. If you get stuck, ask yourself, what's next? When you get an answer, do that."

My paintings that day, and in the weeks to follow, were mostly bold and vibrant. I was totally immersed in the process. It was, as Laura had said, like having a colorful conversation with myself. Student-centered learning, client-centered therapy, and person-centered groups and organizations had been the central stream through my adult life, and here I was in my seventies with a whole new arena in which to learn to be mindful and trust my creative self. Maybe it was a smaller arena, but it was deep.

My engagement in this expressive creative process was making me feel exuberant. I painted one bold geometric face in deep turquoise with bright orangey-red hair and a giraffe-like spotted neck; I later called it my "call to creativity." I flashed back to my decision to retire at sixty. I had hungered for something new. It had been quite a journey, but now it was "aha and hello." I was coming to know a new dimension of myself. I was hearing the language of my soul. My painting was expressing its voice. Upon reflection, it was akin to my experiences thirty years earlier in therapy after I left the school when I learned to feel my body's energy and read the messages of my dreams.

Toward the end of our eight-week series, Laura gave a short talk about using creativity to explore the unknown. With that prompt, as I stood at the paint table, I felt an urge to try colors I hadn't used before. With a brown, orange, gold, and green palette, a tree emerged that later morphed into a tree goddess. Several years later, I would be invited to join a journal writing group that had been meeting in one form or another for many years, guided by Lois Sunrich. Laura was a member of the group. They had named themselves the Tree Goddesses. Although they were two and three decades younger and all so talented as artists, musicians, and writers, I remembered my tree goddess painting and assured myself, *I guess I belong.*

## SoulCollage

Intuitive painting turned out to be the first step in my becoming a Laura devotee. One day, after several eight-week intuitive painting series, she asked me to stay after class.

"I'm going to be offering a class in SoulCollage, a new expressive art modality I've been studying, and I think you would like it."

"What is SoulCollage?" I asked.

"It's a spiritual practice that uses the simple art form of collage. It's a process of intuitively creating a personal deck of collaged cards using magazines and other found images. Each card you make reflects something about yourself, your life, your dreams, and your influences. Your deck of cards together reflects your multifaceted self. It's like creating a personal tarot deck you can use for personal readings, self-exploration, and understanding. It's a process I've been doing for a few years in a training group with the woman who created it," Laura explained.

"Well," I replied, "I know you're a serious Buddhist student and meditator, but I've reached a point in my life where I've stopped reading spiritual books and going to spiritual retreats and teachings or even meditating in a formal way. Back in the eighties, I used the Motherpeace Tarot Deck for personal guidance as I explored feminist spirituality; I even pulled two of those cards to use as the preface and epilogue for my doctoral dissertation. But now I simply want to live my spirituality by trying to be fully present in the moment, every moment." Without my fully realizing it, the expressive arts practices Laura was teaching me, and the experiences I was having with her, were doing just that: teaching me to more deeply connect to my inner experience and be more fully present in the moment, with whatever arose.

I was not really interested in SoulCollage, but Laura was excited about the process, and I trusted and was enthused about Laura, so I signed up. That was over one hundred cards ago. Several friends of mine joined this SoulCollage circle as well, and we became even closer as a result of being on this art and soul journey together.

For over five years, six to eight of us congregated at Laura's home at one o'clock on Tuesday afternoons. Each place at the cloth-covered table was set with a rubber cutting mat and disposable catalog to use for gluing. In the center of the table were containers holding scissors, glue sticks, and X-Acto knives. As we greeted each other with hugs and chitchat, it was tempting to take a peek at the three baskets on the counter containing stacks of magazine pages with images of people, animals, and scenery for backgrounds. A box with drawers contained smaller collage elements: images of flowers, sacred figures, and miscellaneous things like food, clocks, hands, and eyes. In the corner was a stack of 5x7 mat board cards, blue on one side, white on the other, and a packet of transparent envelopes in which to seal each of our cards when we were finished.

We began each session by gathering in Laura's living room where she guided us in meditation to let go of the busyness of our minds and settle into our bodies and the moment. Connecting with our breath and our bodies brought us into a sacred space in which we could sense our connection to our deeper selves and the universe. From this deeper inner space, we each checked in, sharing what was happening in our lives. Then we moved into the SoulCollage process.

Laura instructed us, "Let your intuition guide you, notice what images grab you, and also let your intuition guide you in how to put them together." I did my best to get my mind and my inner critic out of the way, to venture into the unknown and trust the process. As I did, collages would emerge. Sometimes I would find an image that called to me strongly and I mounted it on a card without adding other elements. That "my way" voice has been strong through much of my life. I lean toward the bold, simple, and uncluttered.

After the cards were completed, at the end of each session, we would seek to intuit their meaning as we pondered why we had chosen those images and put them together in that particular way. We sat together and took turns contemplating our cards while saying, "I am the one who . . ." as we stepped into the images and let them speak. We were amazed at what would emerge, at the facets of ourselves that were revealed and the wisdom and knowing our cards held. Sometimes we offered insights into what we saw in each other's cards with statements like, "If this were my card, I think it might be saying . . ." But mostly we witnessed each other's and our own unfolding. It was a sacred process.

Laura explained how the cards in a SoulCollage deck are divided into four suits, just like in tarot and regular card decks. In the beginning, I made "Committee Cards" for aspects of my personality like the critic, the organizer, the part of myself that is vibrant and sexy, and the part who feels vulnerable and alone. For the card I titled "The Warrior," my central image was a picture of a five-year-old girl in a tutu with her arms joined above her head, her feet planted firmly, and a belt around her net skirt, in which a sheathed sword has been placed. I wrote, *I AM ONE WHO:*

- *Carries a sword but keeps it sheathed*
- *Is both powerful and cute*
- *Stands up and reaches for everything she believes is right*

Mounted on the background, I have lips with teeth, encircling her, for which I wrote, *I AM ONE WHO:*

- *Does my own thing, despite others' judgments pro or con*

This warrior who leads the way, despite what others say, was certainly an enduring aspect of my personality.

As time went along, we made "Community Cards" for people who have been important and formative for us, either living or dead, people who we know personally or not. I made cards for my parents and my daughters, for Barbara, Maria, Robert, and other friends, and for Carl Rogers and Ram Dass.

The third suit Laura introduced was the "Companion Suit." In all of the other suits, we could make a limitless number of cards, but in this suit, we made seven cards, one for each of the seven chakras, or energy centers. Laura guided us through a visualization to find a totem animal to represent each chakra. Then we let our intuition guide us to a magazine image to represent the animal that came to us.

When it came time to introduce us to the archetypal dimension of consciousness, the "Council Suit," Laura gave us a fun quiz to help us identify which of the Greek goddess archetypes we most resonated with. I was not surprised to find Artemis, the independent Goddess of the Hunt, dominating my profile, followed by Athena and Aphrodite, all three untethered goddesses. Years before, Jean Shinoda Bolen's book *Goddesses in Everywoman* had introduced me to these goddess archetypes and helped me understand and appreciate that there are many different ways of being a woman instead of judging women as if there were one standard of how to be, a standard defined by the patriarchy. As I created my SoulCollage deck, I felt empowered to make cards for archetypes such as The Light Bearer and The Wise Woman, acknowledging their existence and play in my personality. Making archetype cards allowed me to more fully claim these parts of myself. My Artemis, also known as Diana, The Huntress in Roman mythology, is strong and powerful but holds her bow and arrow at her side, not in a taut shooting stance. Although Artemis in myth is the protector of girls and chastity, mine is vibrant and sexy.

At some point, Laura stopped offering regular SoulCollage classes, but she still got together with us every few months to do SoulCollage readings. We would each formulate a current question: "What guidance do my cards have for me about . . ." then consult our cards and listen to their wisdom. We never ceased to be amazed at the depth of knowing that was revealed, far beyond what our ordinary minds could conceive. I called the women with whom I shared this process my Soul Sisters.

## Visual Journaling

Having experienced how the creation of our SoulCollage cards added such depth to our self-knowing, my Soul Sisters and I were all game when Laura offered to guide us through yet another expressive art experience. Over the course of twelve weeks, we met for four hours each Thursday in Laura's gorgeous garden and studio to explore visual journaling.

This practice is also based on the fundamental principle of process over product. But now, instead of painting on large sheets of paper or creating collages on 5x7 cards, we were working with mixed media in a spiral bound sketchbook. At the start of the first class, Laura excitedly said to us, "Visual journaling is about creative play, y'all! Art journaling is a no-rules creative practice. It's the act of getting out of your head, into your heart, and onto the page. It's the practice of letting go again and again and again . . . and finding yourself in the process. It's about learning to trust and follow our creative impulses and be nourished by our creativity. It is also about creating a *daily* creative practice, making time *every day* to be creative and tap into our creative flow. It's about weaving our creativity into the fabric of our everyday lives."

That first day, the table was set with an 11x14 spiral bound sketchbook and a stack of sheets of wax paper in front of each person. We stood around the table in Laura's back-yard studio. There were no chairs. In the center of the table were large plastic cottage cheese containers filled with different colors of liquid paint. For over an hour, as Laura kept time, we moved around the table, each of us with our journal, making a mark on each page from the first to the last. Quickly, without thinking, we dipped a brush into whatever color the paint container in front of us held, made a mark on our page, inserted a piece of wax paper to keep it from smearing and sticking, turned the page, moved around the table to the next container of paint, and did it again. It was like a dance, all of us moving around the table in syncopated time. Laura called it "christening our journals." It was a practice of letting go, allowing for happy (and sometimes unhappy) accidents, and unabashedly moving into the unknown. This was the beginning.

At home, I was expected to make some mark in my sketchbook every day. We were encouraged to work randomly, jumping around from page to page, using wax paper to keep wet pages from sticking to each other. During the summer while Donna, Jeremy, and my grandsons were visiting, I moved my art supplies and a table into my bedroom from my office/studio, which I turned over to Donna for her online job. On some days while the boys were at day camp, I got lost in my art journal process for hours, using acrylic paint, crayons, Cray-Pas, collage, stamps, stencils, writing, and so many other means of expression, all in a light, free-play way. With permission to paint over anything I didn't like, I built up layers upon layers on my pages. I had thought I was a fairly free spirit, but not being afraid of making a mistake was surprisingly liberating! I loved experimenting. By the end of the twelve weeks, I had established a daily creative practice and filled my journal. All sixty pages were layered with expressions of me. I had created a book of my life! Over the span of a couple years, I enrolled in four separate visual journal series. Knowing the time would come, toward the end of each series, when Laura would instruct us to "pick out the pages you don't like or that don't hold any energy for you and glue them together," gave me even more permission and impetus to experiment—to let out whatever impulse came from inside. This was a wonderful process for people like me who aren't confident in our artistic ability. It made me more courageous in taking creative risks and in trusting my creative impulses.

In one series, Laura asked us to bring in photographs of our ancestors to work with as a theme in our journals. As the only Jewish woman in the group, my reaction was, "Oh well, count me out of this one." I don't have any ancestor photographs. Mine is a fairly common Russian and Eastern European Jewish immigrant story—cut off from our roots with the migration to America that occurred primarily in the three decades around the turn of the twentieth century. I didn't know my grandparents.

I pulled out my parents' photo album from the closet shelf where I'd stashed it when my mom died. It began with two formal bridal pictures: one of my mother by herself and one of my parents together. The rest were snapshots that began on their honeymoon. While both of my grandmothers had been alive when my parents got married, there was not one snapshot of either of them.

I asked my daughters if they had any ancestor photos, and, to my delight, Sharrin came up with a studio photograph of Nettie Goldstein, my buxom paternal grandmother, sitting formal and robust. My father, aged five or six, stood next to her chair with his hand on her shoulder, her little man. I didn't remember ever having seen that photo. I made copies that I used for learning several different photo transfer techniques in my visual journal. As I worked, I felt closer and closer to Nettie Goldstein. As a single immigrant mom, she'd coped with so much. Her husband died of tuberculosis he'd contracted in the terrible working conditions in the sweatshops, leaving her with a three-year-old son, my father, and a six-year-old daughter. Nettie had to put the two of them in an orphanage while she herself went to work in a sweatshop. It took her two years to save enough money to get them out of the orphanage. She opened a little shop with a back room in which they lived, with no indoor plumbing. My father was five when he came out of the orphanage, old enough to go to kindergarten . . . and to work. Early every morning he climbed the elevated subway stairs to get a big bundle of newspapers. He then delivered the newspapers and bottles of milk before he went to school. When my father told me about the orphanage, I exclaimed angrily, "How could your relatives have let that happen? Why didn't your mother's sisters help out?"

My father replied, "Oh, honey, don't be mad at them. They were all so poor. They all had too many mouths to feed themselves."

I've always said I am more like my father than my mother—warm, open, liberal, experimental, always asking, "Why not?" I have a hunch I got those traits from Nettie. As a consequence of my journal process, I felt more deeply connected to my ancestors and also to myself. Nettie's photograph in particular pops up for me surprisingly often now. Although I've had a grounded sense of self for decades, being more connected to Nettie gives me deeper roots.

Laura introduced us to many other expressive devices and

techniques to use in our journals like stamping, stenciling, and Gelli plate printing, but perhaps the element from which I gained the most insight was my own handwriting: large and small, upside-down, sideways, and in a circle. Once legibility was no longer the criteria for judgment, my "awful" scrawl took on new value as my own unique expression. While reac-quainting myself with the pleasure of expressing my thoughts and feelings in written word, I was creating visual elements for layering in my journal. When I look back through my art journals, my specific words and thoughts no longer matter. I experience the joy of letting go.

As I anticipated starting each new visual journal, I had a sense of curiosity, wondering, as I did with SoulCollage, *How will my soul choose to speak to me? What will I learn?* The visual journaling process involved more art making than SoulCollage did, but like SoulCollage, it also tapped into a powerful realm for psycho-spiritual growth. When I look at the sculptures, paintings, and collages I created in my sixties, I feel a sense of delight: *I created that!* Some-times I have a sense of disbelief: *I created that?* But when I look at the four fat art journals I made in my seventies, I see them spilling over with my creative expression, and I feel a deep sense of communion with my essence.

Intuitive painting, SoulCollage, and visual journaling taught me to trust that I am a creative being, able to create from the inside out and pay attention to process over product. Being in these soulful, creative processes with Laura and a precious group of other questing women gave depth, enrich-ment, and meaningful connection to life in my seventies.

In my late thirties and forties, I discovered nude beaches

and learned to let go of inhibitions and be more comfortable with nakedness and my body. Here, decades later, on my expressive art journey, I made myself naked in a new and different way. I exposed myself and became more transparent to my essence. As I neared the completion of my fourth art "book," I realized my daily creative practice had morphed into a desire to write my life.

# BEST FRIEND STILL

October 1-14, 2007

These dates are exact because Barbara made us wonderful journals with a map of Paris for the cover. Barbara had been living in Ashland for three years and was mastering the art of making books, along with enjoying painting and other artistic pursuits. This Paris journal was a treasure. I wished I had more journals like this one to remind me of all the wonderful details of my life.

The Paris journal began: *How do you say "blessed trip" in French? How's this for an auspicious beginning? We got to the San Diego airport at 6 a.m., and the agent offered us upgrades to first class for $500. Barbara's face lit up immediately, but I hesitated. The airline clerk said, "It's an incredible bargain. The price of a one-way ticket is $7,000, and it has full sleepers." Never ones to turn down a bargain, Barbara and I looked at each other, nodded, and said, "Let's go for it!"*

As we polished off our freshly made hot fudge sundaes in first class, served in real glass bowls, not plastic cups, I turned to Barbara and said, "Thanks. Once again you led me into a little indulgence that I wouldn't have allowed myself."

"Maybe so, Suzy, but you've led me on some pretty wild adventures too."

"Like what?"

"How about, 'Let's start a school,' or 'Come to this singles weekend.'"

"Oh yeah, those," I said, laughing. We had a lot of great memories.

When we arrived in Paris, the room we'd booked in a small Left Bank hotel wasn't ready, so we walked down the block to find a café. As we turned the corner, we were in the Place Saint-Michel, and right there was a café overlooking the Seine. While sipping our drinks and congratulating ourselves on our great location, we noticed that across the Pont Saint-Michel on the Île de la Cité, tourists were starting to congregate in the plaza in front of Notre Dame. I don't remember which of us suggested, "Maybe we could slip into the cathedral now, ahead of the crowds." It was a great idea that gave us a lovely, serene start to our time in this magical city.

We walked around the cathedral for a while in awestruck silence. I was almost overwhelmed by its Gothic scale and detail and its centuries and centuries of history. Barbara sat down in a pew, and I joined her. I wondered who else had sat on this bench over time. Had someone sat here during Napoleon's coronation? As I stared up at a magnificent rose window, I slipped into an appreciation of the artistic expression as a glorification of spirit. When we left the cathedral after an hour, Barbara murmured, "I could've sat there all day." She was a better meditator than I was; I was raring to move on.

I always let Barbara navigate wherever we went because she had a great sense of direction and mine was terrible. But, since I'd been in Paris before, I was happy to suggest a daily agenda so we could explore all the highlights of the city—one day the Marais; another the Louvre and a walk through the Tuileries and Right Bank; a day trip to Giverny and another to Montmartre. We viewed all the major impressionist collections and particularly loved L'Orangerie, with its oval-shaped rooms in which we were enveloped by Monet's Water Lilies. We had a perfect sunset cruise on the Bateau Mouche and, of course, lots of browsing around the Left Bank. On a cobblestone alley, we discovered our favorite restaurant, La Jacobine, where we enjoyed an exquisite onion soup and a divine lamb with figs.

And as we neared the end of our perfect Parisian holiday, I was awakened one morning by a surprise phone call from my friend Leyla. She and Daniel had flown in from Istanbul for a busy weekend; we made a date to meet that afternoon on the Île Saint-Louis. She arrived on a bicycle—so Leyla! The bicycle-sharing phenomenon had just started in Paris, way before it hit US cities. Barbara and I had ridden bikes to visit each other when we lived in Tenafly and when we rented houses on Cape Cod in the early seventies, but thirty-five years later, we were much happier to walk the streets of Paris. Leyla took us to an utterly delightful shop on the Île for the most delectable hot chocolate I'd ever tasted. The shop was a little girl's fantasyland populated by fairies and witches hanging from the ceiling. We spent a delicious, sweet hour together, then Leyla had to rush off. Barbara and I spent the rest of the afternoon shopping. It was fun to mix friends from different aspects of my life, just as I enjoyed being with Barbara's two childhood friends from New York and her friends from Oregon.

Barbara and I had a trip to South America planned for the following year, but the recession of 2008 changed all that. And though my international travel days ended shortly thereafter, Barbara and I still made it a point to get together several times a year in San Diego, Berkeley, and Ashland. Every spring I attended the Ashland Film Festival. None of her other friends binged with her as I did, willing to watch four or five films a day for all five days of the festival.

———

I loved spending time with her daughter, Joanne, and her grandchildren too. Barbara generously shared her "grandmothering" with me until I had grandchildren of my own. I have sweet memories of her first grandchild, Jack, as a toddler in Berkeley, dressed in full fireman's regalia, climbing into their dog Casey's bed to pretend nap. I was also the second set of grandmother arms to hold twins Rachel and Ben when they were born. One year, when their kids were little, Joanne and her husband, Jeff, invited us to join them for a week in Maui. Barbara and I expected to babysit so they could get some couple's vacation time. Unfortunately, Barbara became sick on the airplane with an awful respiratory bug, and I got it by the next morning, along with a bad ear infection. So instead of babysitters, Joanne and Jeff ended up with three little kids and two nanas to tend. Along with antibiotic shots, the doctor actually wrote out a prescription for us for pho from a specific restaurant—the Vietnamese version of the Jewish chicken soup on which we were raised. The frequency of my trips to Ashland, Barbara's trips to San Diego and Riverside, where one of her sons and his family live, and both of our trips to the Bay Area, where three of our children and their partners live, gave us a wonderful multi-layered bond with each other's children and grandchildren. We were all on the West Coast for about forty years, so my daughters' lives were more intertwined with Barbara and her family than with their East Coast aunts and cousins, my brother's family, and Myles's clan. And then there was the fact that all but the youngest of our combined seven children went from nursery school through high school together.

———

In addition to our intertwined family and history, and all the ways we have been there for each other, it was often sharing the simplest things that we did best. As we entered our third act, Barbara and I still talked on the phone all the time, but it was no longer an absolute everyday occurrence. However, we were both addicted to the computer game Words with Friends and often had multiple games going with each other simultaneously. Consequently, when a game from Barbara flashed on my iPad screen, I would say to myself, *Oh, Barbara just got up*, or *Wow, Barbara's up late.*

I observed, yes, somewhat judgmentally, the degree to which electronic devices keep people from being present with each other or with the environment as they talk on their cell phones, play games, or check texts, tweets, email, and Facebook. Yet I acknowledge Barbara and I engaged in a version of the same thing, in some ways even more impersonally— staying connected through our games with no verbal communication whatsoever beyond an occasional chat room *"I've got all vowels!"*

Over the fifty-plus years since we met, we've participated together and separately in encounter groups at the school and elsewhere, then singles groups after we got divorced, and Core Energetic/Pathwork psycho-spiritual groups in New York. Once we moved to California, we continued exploring together in women's groups, new age groups, and then Buddhist spiritual groups and art classes. It has been a rare gift to have a friend with whom to grow and share, support and reflect.

In her memoir, author Ann Patchett talks about someone characterizing a happy marriage by asking, "Does your husband make you a better person?" I would unequivocally say that Barbara has made me a better person. For me, as my best friend, she has always been, and continues to be, an incredible life partner.

We also continued to have fun. In the sixth decade of our friendship, our mutual interests still ranged from the sacred to the profane. A few years ago, we walked by Good Vibrations in Berkeley by chance, so, of course, we went in. We were enticed by their sleek Italian displays. Maybe we're both just creatures of habit, but when we subsequently compared notes on our vibrator purchases, we both felt that the shiny new battery-operated stuff just didn't measure up to our old plug-in clunkers. They were not hip or sexy, and we hated to admit that now we only needed to replace them every decade or two, no longer purchased from Bloomingdale's, but from the "Massagers" section of the local drugstore. What matters, we both agreed, was that they worked! During our last conversation about this, I was reminded of that day in Mykonos, lying on the beach and feeling open enough to talk about my sexuality for the first time, and I realized, despite all of the women friends I have known and cherished, there is no one beside Barbara with whom I would have had this conversation.

Some years ago, after her ear tumor surgery and my eye diseases, Barbara joked, "When we're old, we will arrive at a street corner, and I will ask, 'Can we cross? Do you hear anything?' And you will reply, 'I think so. Do you see anything?' And then we'll look at each other and ask, 'Why are we crossing the street?'"

In fact, that joke held our shared expectation that we would end up living next door to each other in Berkeley someday. Berkeley was chosen as a compromise because I didn't want to move to Ashland and Barbara didn't want to come back to San Diego. An additional driver of this decision was the fact that three of our children who live in the Bay Area encouraged us to move near them. Neither of us would want to live with our children, which I'm sure our children feel good about. Barbara and I also realized we each liked living alone; next door to each other sounded perfect.

To this day, occasionally Barbara will say, "Berkeley?" and I'll reply, "Not yet." Neither of us is ready to move. We're both grounded in the now. She has her subscription to the symphony and the Shakespeare Theater, and I have mine to the Old Globe. We each have our circles of friends and our passions: bookmaking for her, writing for me. One of us will say, "Is it irresponsible of us not to make plans?" and the other will reply, "I have no idea what the future will be. I can only live in the present." Then both of us will say in unison, "Don't you dare die first!"

# FULL CIRCLE

January 2011

*I want to wake up in Paris on my seventy-fifth birthday.* It didn't matter that I had spent two weeks in Paris with Barbara in 2007 and then stopped international traveling altogether after the recession of 2008. It didn't matter that Paris would probably be freezing cold, maybe snowy and awful. On January 13, 2011, I wanted to wake up in Paris. It was a last hurrah, and I wanted it to be with my daughters. Sharrin couldn't come because she'd just had surgery. I wasn't willing to postpone until she recuperated. As much as I loved her, I wanted to wake up in Paris ON my birthday, not a few months later.

Of course, Wendy would come. Even married and coping with severe health challenges, she was always game to go anywhere. Within her cycle of monthly lumbar punctures to relieve her high-pressure headaches, we had managed several museum/theater binges in New York and London and four other international trips: a tour of Egypt and Petra; a wedding in Istanbul followed by a sailing excursion on the Aegean; a jaunt to Madrid, Bilbao, and Barcelona; and, most important of all, my seventieth birthday trip to Australia, Fiji, and New Zealand, where she met David.

I was thrilled that Donna could come to Paris too. I had not traveled alone with her for over twenty-five years. As a young woman, while her sisters and I went to various places, Donna always chose to go to Paris to see her friends Gilles and Patrick. But the last time she had visited them was with her husband, Jeremy, when Julian was one year old. She had lost touch with "the boys" except for the annual Christmas card exchange. So, approaching 2011, with Julian ten and a half and Kai seven and a half, when I extended the invitation to Paris, Jeremy said yes. Yes, he could manage the boys so Donna could go. He also added, only partly joking, "There'd be no living with her otherwise." I felt grateful that Donna had an online job so that she and her family could spend Christmas and summer vacations with me, but it was special to be alone with her and together with Wendy as three adult women.

On the flight over, I pulled out my iPad to dig into the novel I had downloaded, but I didn't open it right away. My mind flipped back through my own story—to my first solo flight to Europe when I flew to Spain to celebrate my divorce in 1977 when I was forty-one.

Back then, I was asking myself, *Can I make it in the big world on my own?* I laughed to myself with a little smile and a big head roll. *Yes! I did it! Beyond my wildest dreams! My post-divorce chapter has been incredible.* I felt so grateful, so pleased with myself, but also sad. I was okay that this was my final trip to Europe. I'd been there almost every year for over twenty years. I was sad because it was unlikely I would see my wonderful European friends again.

*But,* I reassured myself, *when one door closes, another one opens. I'm in a new chapter, with more focus on my inner landscape. Ha, funny I should think of my inner landscape just as we're off to binge on our favorite landscape artist.* I loved that this "we" included Wendy and Donna, my two favorite Monet fans. (With Sharrin, I enjoyed more contemporary art.) Our "primo" destination was the special Monet show at the Petit Palais, the largest Monet exhibit ever mounted.

Once I knew we were going to Paris, I emailed Leyla: "Could you fly in from Istanbul for any part of my birthday week?"

She replied, "I'm so sorry, I can't come that week. We've already got a commitment in Istanbul that we can't change. But guess what? We're in Paris right now because we just bought a fabulous apartment in the 5th arrondissement, right near the Pantheon. We're here furnishing it. We can't be here that week, but you and the girls are welcome to stay here."

The apartment was fabulous—decorated with Leyla's creative flair, including a sleek undersized bright green toilet and sink in the typically Parisian tiny bathroom. When I awakened the first morning and stumbled to the bathroom, I found the sink filled with birthday cards, including one they'd brought from Sharrin. Wendy and Donna had given me permission to awaken them so we could get started early. In honor of my birthday, they overcame their usual morning demands for silence. We dressed and left quickly for breakfast.

Donna said, "I'm salivating at the thought of French coffee and my first croissant."

"Me too," I replied. "I haven't had a croissant since my last trip to Paris."

"Wait a minute, Mom. What about those twelve-packs we buy at Costco when Jeremy, the boys, and I are visiting you?"

"Haven't you noticed? They sit on top of my refrigerator while you all work your way through them, but I never indulge. However, what I stick to as healthy eating at home would be sacrilegious in Paris."

I don't remember whether it was Wendy or Donna who said, "Ma-ahm, zip it. We don't want to hear you talk about food or weight. We're in Paris." I zipped it; I knew better. I'd talked too much about dieting and food when they were growing up. I needed to keep my self-monitoring monologue to myself.

Much to our delight, as we approached the Boulevard Saint-Michel, we spotted a café with outdoor tables across from the Luxembourg Gardens. No one was sitting outside. It was January. But we looked at each other and nodded in unison. "Here." Donna volunteered, "I'll go in and ask if they'll serve us outside."

I turned to Wendy. "I can't believe it's warm enough to sit out here and people-watch while we have our breakfast. I heard they had a blizzard last week. Are you really warm enough only wearing a sweater?"

"You know my wacky thermostat, Mom."

Donna returned with a smile and said the waiter would be right out.

As we waited for our breakfast, I said, "I was here on my honeymoon. Did I tell you about that?"

"TMI!" they said in unison.

"No, no. I was just going to tell you that your father and I stayed in a little hotel, near here on the Boulevard Saint-

Germain. Our room looked out on the Luxembourg Gardens. When we went out for breakfast the first morning, we ordered croissants, and the waiter brought us a basket full. I'd never had a croissant before. It was so divine, I gobbled it up, then had another, as you know I can do, eating too fast. Your father took his third, and so did I. When the waiter brought the check, your father's eyes popped. In New York, they don't usually charge for bread, but if they do, it's a flat charge because the health law requires them to discard what's left in the bread basket. But in Paris, they charge by how many you eat. We blew our *Europe on a $10 a Day* budget that very first day."

"Ten dollars a day? How much was your hotel room?" asked Donna.

"Oh, three or four dollars. I don't remember exactly; I found it in Frommer's guidebook. We used the same book all through Europe."

"But Mom, you can't exactly call it a budget honeymoon when you were driving around in a Mercedes."

"You're right, Wendy. When we left Paris, we picked up the Mercedes your father had ordered. It wasn't like *your* budget travel in Europe and Asia."

"Mine either," reminisced Donna. "Before I started visiting Gilles and Patrick, my trip with my friends Meg and Sharon in college was super budget."

"Did you ever stay at Shakespeare and Company?" Wendy asked Donna.

"You bet. You too?"

"I wonder if he's still alive and how the bookstore is doing. It's not too far. Let's check it out while we're here."

When the waiter delivered our breakfast, we inhaled in unison. While Wendy busied herself preparing her tea, Donna and I took our first sips of coffee, put croissants on our plates, and sniffed their luscious, buttery scent. I ripped off a tip and took my first flaky bite. I think I closed my eyes for a moment as I savored the yumminess. Then the big decision: Should I add some butter and jam? *Slow down,* I told myself. *You're only going to eat one. And don't say anything; just set a good example.*

I took another sip of my coffee. It was perfect. I looked around and said, "Forever after, when I wake up on my birthday, I will remember sitting outside this café with you two. But now, let's finish up and get going."

Anxious to get to the Monet show and wanting to preserve Wendy's energy, I suggested, "As enticing as it might be to meander across the Seine, let's take a cab straight to the Petit Palais."

Donna and I groaned when we saw the admission line snaking out of sight. But Wendy piped up, "See that short line for museum members? That's us. Follow me." She had anticipated the crowds and had joined the museum in advance. For non-members it must have been at least a three-hour wait. *Bravo, Wendy!*

When we got inside, the exhibition was already mobbed. Who said it first? "I hate crowded museums." I like to get up close to paintings and move back and forth and sideways at my own pace. Instead, we pushed our way into the stream and surrendered to the crowd as it moved us along. I didn't mind the relatively quick pace through the first rooms because the paintings were so realistic, with none of the shimmering light I associate with Monet.

I said to Wendy, "Are you sure these are Monets and not Manets?"

"No, Mom. It's like the shock we had in Barcelona when we went to the Picasso Museum and saw his totally realistic paintings from high school. This is quite a collection of Monet's early work. It's going to be fun to watch his evolution."

"If we can see it with this crowd."

I don't remember specific paintings, just the overall subtle color feast and gorgeous hazy light he captured in all the seasons. After an hour and a half, Donna and I were glassy-eyed and insisted that Wendy take a break with us "NOW." We were fortunate to score a table in the quiet museum café for lunch instead of the noisy cafeteria. After giving our eyes and feet a rest, we went back to continue to the end of the exhibit. Altogether, it was more than a three-hour binge. As my macular degeneration progresses, I will hold Monet's paintings as a reminder of how beautiful the world can be when the details are fuzzy. I knew I would need to adopt "softer and gentler" as my way of being.

One night, I led Wendy and Donna through the charming streets of Saint-Germain to La Jacobine, the restaurant Barbara and I had discovered in a cobblestone alley. Knowing my poor sense of direction, my daughters were skeptical, but they tried to indulge me because it was my birthday trip. When I actually found the place, we were all relieved. They loved the casual ambiance as much as I did. As a pescatarian, Donna used a slice of bread to mop up the last drop of garlicky butter sauce from her mussels. Wendy acknowledged, "Mom you were right, the lamb with figs was divine."

There was something so satisfying about having my own little discovery to recommend—a tiny bit of an illusion of "knowing" Paris instead of the truth: I was just a tourist. But I liked proving I'm capable. *Is that my insecurity,* I wondered, *or is there something in my daughters' behavior that makes me feel I need to prove my competence?*

Browsing in Parisian shops is always fun, but this time was particularly wonderful because it was the week of the semi-annual sales. I learned from my mother and passed on to my daughters an energetic response to "Sale" signs. In a shop in the Marais, I stopped to look at something as Wendy and Donna walked on ahead. As I followed them into another room, I spotted the sale rack, missed an unmarked step, and fell. My depth perception and peripheral vision were not very good anymore, so I was super careful, but show me a "Sale" sign and uh-oh.

A man waiting for his wife helped me up, noting that others had missed that step too, which made me feel a little better, but not much. I wasn't physically hurt, but my pride was so damaged I felt like crying. The store, in typical French fashion, took no responsibility. No one asked if I was okay or offered me a glass of water or a seat. We left with Wendy saying, "Oh, Mom, I'm so sorry," over and over again, as if it were her responsibility to be my seeing eye dog. After this event, she would point out every crack in the sidewalk and every curb wherever we were.

That day, though, we were on a hunt for the perfect French jacket for Sharrin. We found one that afternoon. I said, "That orangey color will look great with her auburn hair." Donna nodded, "She'll love the style." Wendy added,

"And it's the perfect weight for Bay Area winters." While they were wrapping up the jacket, I tried on a coat I loved, but I didn't buy it.

The girls chatted as they walked in front of me through the Marais, while I listened to this punitive voice inside me saying, *You don't deserve that coat, you klutz!* Tears started to slip out, and I couldn't control them. My sense of vitality and competence was shaken, maybe shattered.

When we arrived at the main thoroughfare, they saw I was upset.

"Mom, what's wrong?" they asked.

I explained how vulnerable and angry at myself I was, and Donna commanded, "Wendy, you go sit down at that café to wait for us. Mom and I are walking back to that shop to buy her that coat." It was a sign of the compassion I needed to ex- tend to myself, much as I would have given to my daughters, clients, or friends. For the rest of the week in Paris, I wore the coat every day and felt very chic. Reflecting back on this later, I would see . . . this was a celebration of the end of my travel- ing days, and doing this with my daughters was, in a manner of speaking, coming full circle.

Upon my return to San Diego, I wore the black wool coat with purple, gray, and white circles on it every time I went to the theater in the winter. Remembering the joys far more than the fall, I loved saying, "Oh, thank you. I bought it on a trip to Paris with my daughters to celebrate my seventy-fifth birthday."

# THE ORGAN RECITAL

September 2012

When we were younger (in our fifties and sixties!), my friends and I used to roll our eyes and mutter, "Oh, here comes the organ recital," when older people started all conversations with their litany of aches and pains and physical ailments. Suddenly, in September of 2012, at age seventy-six, I found myself with a starring role in the same recital.

### First Movement:
### The Day I Went Blind in My Good Eye

As I headed downstairs in my condo to make my morning coffee, I realized, uncharacteristically, that I had a headache, not in my whole head, just around my right eye. Coffee didn't help, so I took two Tylenol.

*Is the vision in my right eye a little blurry?* I asked myself.

*No,* I answered. *It just seems that way because it's foggy outside.*

By 8:30 a.m., I decided something really did seem off. *The fog is inside me, not a marine layer over the beach.*

I looked at my suitcase—all packed with black pants and black tops for my New York museum/theater binge with Wendy. I was leaving early the next morning, so to be on the safe side, I told myself, *I'll make an appointment to get my eyes checked out this afternoon.*

But first, I wanted to go to my new memoir class. The daily practice of working in my art journals had turned into a desire to start writing about my life, and then this memoir class had appeared. I explained to Lois Sunrich, the teacher, that I wanted to participate, but I needed to get to this urgent eye appointment. It was okay with her for me to step in and out of the room until I got it settled.

It took several phone calls to the Shiley Eye Institute, and my insistence that I must be seen in the face of much resistance: "Your doctor is not in today." "You were just here last Friday." "We're all booked today." I wouldn't give up. I insisted, "There's something wrong with my eye. I must be seen today. If you can't schedule an appointment for me, let me speak to whatever doctor is on duty." The more I insisted, the more I convinced myself there was something wrong. Finally, I got an okay to show up at Dr. Katibbi's clinic at one o'clock.

Relieved to have the appointment, I was able to get into the writing assignment in class. But, when we took a bathroom break, I realized that the fog in my right eye had become more like a dirty windshield. I was frightened and couldn't stop closing one eye and then the other to check what was happening. I don't have much vision remaining in my left eye due to macular degeneration and glaucoma, so I was comparing to be sure I could still see better out of my right eye. With a shaky hand, I tried to call my friend Liv.

On the third try, I dialed correctly. Thank God, she was home. I asked her to drive me to Shiley. Liv heard the panic in my voice and reorganized her schedule so she could take me. Relieved I had a plan, I went back and finished the memoir class. Then I drove myself home, which wasn't the smartest thing to do with my dirty windshield vision.

An hour later at Shiley, the tech said, "Cover your left eye, and read the eye chart." I saw nothing—no big *E*, no eye chart. Nothing. I freaked. My breath stopped. My throat clenched shut with panic. The early morning fog had progressed to total blackness in my good eye. I finally got the words out: "I'm blind. I can't see a thing."

Magdalena, the sweet tech, tried to soothe me. "Don't worry, I'll get the doctor right away."

Dr. Katibbi looked into my eye and told me, "It's filled with debris from a massive eye infection." She assumed I'd gotten it three days earlier from my regular eye injections. Along with the blindness, she informed me the infection had caused my eye pressure to be at a dangerous 38, way up from the 12-15 range maintained by my twice daily glaucoma drops. She explained she would immediately remove the fluid from my eye to get the pressure down, then she would give me a massive shot of antibiotics directly into my eye.

"This," she warned me, "will be unpleasant." I gripped the arms of the chair and white knuckled through it with no more than a high-pitched "ummmm" as I held my breath, keeping my mouth shut and my head still. After the procedure, she checked my pressure again, and it had shot up to 80. I white knuckled it again as she quickly removed more fluid and got the pressure under control.

The good news, I was told, was that we caught it so early. The incubation period for an infection from the shot is seventy-two hours. Because I paid attention to those first signs, I actually received the antibiotics shot seventy hours after that bugger slipped in with my Eylea injection. Dr. K said it happens in one of every 1500 to 2000 shots, despite sterilization precautions. *Lucky me!* Because only one eye was infected, and I had shots in both eyes, it clearly was not caused by the medication; it must have been "insufficient sterilization of the site." Never again would I complain about how much the Betadine disinfectant burns!

Dr. Katibbi explained she would send the fluid to be cultured. We would have to wait to know whether it was a staph or a strep infection before we could know what to do next.

A few hours later, my daughter Sharrin arrived from Oakland to take care of me. We ended up needing to go back to Shiley almost every day for a week, even Saturday and Sunday. I don't remember what symptoms I was having, but the Shiley docs weren't taking any chances.

A few days after it happened, Sharrin suggested we go for pedicures. I said, "Okay. There's a place at Cardiff Town Center. Let's walk there." I wanted to prove to myself and to her that I could see well enough out of my other eye to walk, including navigating the traffic light and street crossing. She was the perfect person to let me do it. Wendy and Donna would have been too overprotective to let me cross the street without holding on to me.

But, once inside the hip nail salon with big screens playing rock videos, I felt old and fragile. I couldn't see well enough to pick out a hot nail polish color, so I settled for something conservative. I couldn't muster the energy to sustain a conversation with the manicurist, so I pretended to watch the video, but I couldn't engage with that either. My head was spinning with frightened thoughts of, *Oh my God, what's happened to me?* and *Oh my God, what's going to happen to me?* By the time we got to lunch across the patio from the nail spa, tears dripped down my cheeks.

I explained to Sharrin, "I aged twenty years in a moment. I went from feeling like a competent, vital young senior, at least ten years younger than my real age, to at least ten years older than I am. I feel like a frail eighty-six-year-old."

"Oh, Mom," she said. "No wonder you're upset. You're not only in the sudden shock of not seeing, but you're on a big dose of prednisone, which I'm sure is taking you for an emotional roller-coaster ride. You said you're not sleeping well, and I can see you're ravenous. Welcome to my world of steroid hell."

I had a new appreciation of Sharrin's and Wendy's challenges with steroid use for their health problems. I was experiencing how finely wired and chemically tuned we are—and therefore, how susceptible we are to changes in our chemical balance.

Understanding the steroid effect helped. It was like when I had bouts of tears as a young woman, and then I'd get my period and say, "Aha! That's why I'm so miserable. My hormones are acting up." But menstrual period or prednisone, I still felt awful and teary.

As we went through that first week, Sharrin commented, "Never did I think I'd be hoping to hear a doctor say, 'You've got a staph infection.'" But staph infection it turned out to be, which meant that the antibiotic shot had killed it. We were told, "There's a good chance the debris will eventually clear without surgery. Had it been a strep infection, it would have been a whole different story involving not only surgery but possible permanent damage and vision loss."

I was very fortunate.

The biggest blessing of all was that it happened on Monday and, because I was going away on Tuesday, I dealt with it immediately. Had I awakened on Tuesday morning with the same symptoms, I probably would have taken the Tylenol and gone off to the airport. All the chief doctors and fellows and residents at Shiley told me that what saved my eye was the immediate antibiotic shot. What a lesson this was: where my health is concerned, it's important to pay attention to the small stuff.

As I walked along the shoreline on my daily walk, I closed one eye and then the other, over and over again, hoping my right eye would go back to showing me more than my left. Not yet, but I asked myself, *Could you live with this? If this is all you had, could you live with this?* I reminded myself of my Monet binge in Paris two years earlier with Wendy and Donna for my seventy-fifth birthday. *Blurry is beautiful,* I had told myself. *You could live with this.*

Over the course of a few months, I regained my vision with no permanent damage from the staph infection. I didn't need any eye surgery. I breathed a sigh of relief. Once I knew I would get better, I told myself, *This is a dress rehearsal for the time when your macular degeneration and glaucoma get worse.* When I wrote about those months, I titled the chapter "Blinded, but not Blindsided."

## Second Movement: A Matched Set—In Titanium

Once I stopped checking on my vision, I wasn't done taking a body inventory. I am not a gym person, a yoga devotee, or a swimmer. I walk the beach every day for an hour. At seventy-six, some days I would groan as I sat to tie my sneakers; other days I walked a block or two before I said, "Ugh, my left knee," or "Ugh, my right hip," or "Ow, my groin muscle," or "Oh, shit, my lower back is in a knot; I hope it loosens up quickly." I called the litany "my floating crap game." Some part of my lower body was always hurting. It varied from day to day or week to week. I took Celebrex daily and went for acupuncture regularly, massages occasionally, and cortisone shots or physical therapy once in a while. Such was the case when I called my orthopedist in December of 2012. I was about to turn seventy-seven.

Holding up the X-ray, Dr. Hajnik pointed, "See all that flaky stuff? That's arthritis; your knee is riddled with it. And see these two bones; there's no meniscus cushion left in between. You're bone on bone. How much is the pain interfering with your daily life?"

I nodded my head from side to side and admitted, "It's difficult and sometimes impossible for me to take my daily beach walk or sit with my knee bent through a two-hour movie or play."

"If it's interfering with your daily life, it's time to replace it."

I took a deep breath, grimaced, and nodded. "Yes," I said as I exhaled slowly. To myself I said, *Oh, shit. Knee replacement surgery again. Last time it took a whole year of pain and rehab, and I was seven years younger then.*

This time, I didn't remember anything after the surgery at the hospital. For three days I was in a fog of pain and pain meds. *Did I have a roommate? Did they really get me standing up? Did I walk to the bathroom? Nah, I must have just used a bedpan.* When I was discharged, I remember being rolled from my bed onto a gurney with the help of two nice EMT guys. But once they rolled me into the ambulance, they chatted with each other up front while they drove me like a sack of potatoes in the back. They were delivering me from the hospital in Encinitas to the rehab wing of Silverado, a senior residence in Del Mar. I didn't like being rolled in lying down. I felt so helpless and anonymous.

I was transferred from the gurney onto a bed. It hurt to move. I was exhausted by the effort. My doctor's office had recommended I buy an ice machine, and they'd shipped it with me from the hospital. Someone hooked me up by wrapping my knee in the bandage with embedded coils through which icy water ran continuously to keep the swelling down. An aide filled the bucket with ice every few hours. I dozed, awakened, asked for pain meds, and dozed again. In between, I was in a fog, but I was clear enough to say to myself, *This is awful.*

I had chosen to come to Silverado because they offered intense daily physical therapy with exercise equipment as well as daily occupational therapy to learn techniques for dressing, maneuvering stairs, etc. Had I chosen to go straight home, the physical therapy wouldn't have been as frequent or as intense for the first two weeks. After that, I would be eligible for an outpatient physical therapy clinic.

Michelle, the physical therapist, was young and pretty, with curly light brown hair and a great big smile. I liked her immediately. "I hear you ordered a continuous motion machine. Awesome. You'll make much faster progress with that." I liked her positive, encouraging attitude.

The worst part of my daily PT sessions was when she had me stretch out and then she pushed my lower leg into the back of my thigh to measure my degree of flexion. "The goal is to get you to 120 degrees eventually. Let's see how close we can get you to 90 degrees when you leave here." I liked the concrete measurable goal, but the daily push hurt like hell. My eyes got watery, but I took a deep breath in and let it out slowly without uttering a peep as she bent my knee more and more each day.

We passed the dining room on the way back from PT to my room. It sounded like a noisy sociable restaurant, but I was glad I had arranged for all my meals on a tray in my room. I wasn't there to socialize. I sat down on the bed and strapped the ice bandage around my knee. Michelle picked up the metal-framed continuous motion machine and placed it in my bed. She warned me not to try to pick it up myself; it was much too heavy for me to handle with my precarious balance.

Michelle showed me how to buckle my thigh into position and turn on the machine. She set the range of motion and encouraged me to increase it a little every day and use it for six hours a day. I liked that my new knee was being exercised without my having to do anything except endure being strapped in. I hated being immobilized, but I wasn't up to running around anyway. I got antsy when the nurse was late delivering my meds—I kept close tabs on that. My modus operandi: *Stay ahead of the pain. I'll deal with withdrawal from the drugs when I'm ready.*

On the first day, as I held on to a railing along the hallway wall and slowly walked myself back from the physical therapy room, I had an upsetting experience. It was a little later in the morning than when I'd been taken in the wheelchair. Breakfast was over. The dining room was empty. But outside in the hall was a line of wheelchairs. All occupied. Filled with old people with vacant stares—waiting to be wheeled back to their rooms, then wheeled out again for the next meal.

*Do they enjoy their food? Do they enjoy sitting in their wheelchairs? Do they know where they are? Is that old age? I never want to end up like that. NEVER!* I turned my head to avoid making eye contact. Their helplessness inspired me to stick to my exercise regime every day no matter how much my knee hurt. *I don't want to end up like that—vacant in a wheelchair.*

When I got moved into a single room, I celebrated by digging into the tote bag in my little closet. Inside I had stashed a thermos filled with my favorite cabernet. I didn't drink a lot— after all, I was on pain meds. But, at my request, my friend Judy had slipped me some wine when I'd had my first knee replaced, so I knew I'd do well with a nightly toast to my healing. When my supply got low, I asked her to refill my thermos.

After two weeks, Wendy came to take me home. I had an appointment with Dr. Hajnik. He pushed my shin into my thigh to measure my flexion and said, "Good for you. You're at 90 degrees. You can return the continuous motion machine. It stops at 90. Now it's up to you to try with PT to get to 120."

A week later, I tried to start writing:

*2/4/13 Checking to see if I can write while on these meds. I keep sorta dozing. Okay, it's 2:38 p.m. We'll see what happens. Oops. I can't even control my fingers, no less my eyelids and my brain. I keep nodding . . .*

*4/19/13 Just read that entry in February. No wonder I stopped writing. I really couldn't. I dropped everything to focus on rehab. Here I am, exactly three months after my surgery and doing so well. Yesterday Dr. Hajnik pulled out his plastic measuring device and said, "Bend your knee. Bravo! You made it to a full 120 degrees flexion. You're discharged. See you in two years for a checkup."*

He was done, but I was not. It took another nine months of work: traditional PT, then a more holistic PT that worked on my whole-body alignment and balance, plus acupuncture and daily beach walking. By the time my seventy-eighth birthday arrived, I was in better shape physically than I remember being in my entire adult life. I resolved, again, to continue to move and maintain my physical shape as much as I could for as long as I could. I was a latecomer to physical exercise; I didn't really start until I moved to California at age forty-six. However, my body forgave me for past neglect and strain, and it continued to reward me as long as I kept walking. Once more, I was reminded, it's never too late . . .

# NEW PASSION

Fall 2013

When the Student Is Ready . . .

If I'd needed a motivator to make a leap into a new purpose-fulness, the sight of those vacant elders in their wheelchairs at the senior facility would qualify as the stimulus. But I was already bitten by the writing bug from the moment I started in Lois Sunrich's memoir class on what turned out to be the first day of my organ recital. By the time I recuperated from my bout with blindness and my knee replacement, I was raring to go. In a writing workshop, Lois gave the prompt, "I am a woman who . . ." and I continued, "had the courage to move to California." I was off and running.

Lois mentored me every step of the way from the initial "let your pen do the walking," to guiding and supporting me as I rambled on and on, writing my life story. Lois called this "laying down the tracks." I also joined her monthly journal-writing group, Tree Goddesses. The Trees are all extraordi-narily talented women, two decades or more younger than I, and our roots have become deeply intertwined.

As a coach, Lois knew when to push me out of the nest. When I was ready to start learning how to sculpt my story into a coherent entity, she encouraged me to start taking writing classes at San Diego Writers, Ink, a nonprofit organization for writers based at Liberty Station, the same locale where I'd started my art/spirit connection with Laura Hansen earlier in my seventies.

One Saturday morning, I signed up for a class entitled "Finding Your Voice," taught by Marni Freedman. I think it was love at first sight! I resonated immediately with Marni's feisty "out there" energy, which I heard as New York Jewish. It turned out she was LA Jewish. Despite the thirty-odd-year age difference, we are kindred spirits.

I told her, "I've written the first draft of my memoir, and now I want to learn the craft of making my writing more readable. I'm looking for a weekly read and critique group."

She said, "I think I'm going to have an opening in my Encinitas group. Where do you live?"

I rolled my eyes and grinned from ear to ear as I answered, "How's that for 'When the student is ready, the teacher will appear.' I am in Cardiff, less than five minutes from downtown Encinitas."

I gave Marni my first draft. After reading it, she said, "You have at least three memoirs in here." Since she is also a licensed therapist, she was excited about my writing about my connections to Carl Rogers and my career at CSP. She thought that would be the most easily publishable part of my story.

But I told her, "I'm fulfilled from the two wonderful careers I've had, so I have no need for further accomplishment in the outside world. I feel no pressure to publish, just to write. I want to write my life story and my family's history for my daughters and future ancestors, and I want to learn how to write well."

Marni gave me permission to include all the details in the autobiography instead of whittling the totality down to one theme for a memoir. The dozen wonderful women in our weekly read and critique group, all exceedingly talented writers, gave me a free pass for being such a beginner in learning the craft. I was decades older than most of them, and with those years brought the wisdom of more experience with life. The group was called The Feisty Writers, and from the start, I knew I was qualified, even inspired, in the "feisty" department; it was the "writer" part I had to work on. I appreciated the other Feisties' patience and help enormously. I sat entranced as they read their writing, loved what I was doing, and felt the momentum to keep moving forward. It was wonderful being so involved and purposeful. It felt like I was embarking on my third career.

Even now, I wake up every morning looking forward to sitting in my tan leather chair and getting to work, opening my laptop to review the previous day's writing before moving on. Although my daughters have not expressed any great interest in reading my story (after all, they lived it with me and sometimes were victims of it), The Feisty Writers have been interested and supportive throughout. When I completed the 700-page first draft, they suggested I divide it into two volumes, and then members of the group edited both volumes.

Then one day, I took another leap. I announced: "I'm going to leave my two-volume autobiography on my computer. Someday, I'll polish it and print it for my family, but

I've decided to write a memoir." They were so incredibly encouraging as I plodded on, still far from mastering the principle of "show, don't tell."

The intellectual part has been fun. I enjoyed coming up with a theme and picking stories from my life to illustrate the theme. I started with Marni's hero's journey structure but eventually realized that, for me, I never quite fit the mold in my life, so in writing my memoir I would need to find my own theme and structure.

The writing itself was a journey. Every day, I sat in my leather writing chair, put a pillow on my lap, then my turquoise lap desk, and then maneuvered my silky silver laptop onto the top of the stack so the screen would be as close to my eyes as possible. I opened my computer and typed in my code. Usually what I'd been working on the day before popped right up for review. When I was done editing, I'd put in my chapter heading and the date, and then . . . sometimes I'd just hit a wall. I would be all psyched up to begin writing a new chapter, but I would clutch, someplace in my chest. I knew I wanted to create a scene and come up with dialogue, but I couldn't find the words. So, I would reread my outline, get up and pee, sit back down and take a sip of water, look out the sliding glass doors, come back to the glowing white screen, rest my fingers on the black keyboard, and order myself, "Start typing."

If the phone rang, I didn't answer it. This was my writing time.

Every once in a while, I would get a poke from my Apple watch, commanding me to "Stand up!" *Have I really been sitting and writing for an hour?* I would ask myself. Often, I didn't feel like stopping, so I wouldn't. I'd get another poke and think, *Has another hour really passed? Just a little bit more.* I felt the pull to finish my story in time to reduce the draft to 12-point type from my 16-point comfort level so I could squeeze it into the eight-page limit to read to The Feisties. I hadn't necessarily mastered the art of writing, but at least I'd mastered the basics of my computer, printer, and stapler.

Thursdays became the best day of the week. It was the day I met with The Feisty Writers. Either Elizabeth or Kim, who lived nearby, would pick me up for the five-minute ride to Barb's house. I had my spot, next to Nancy on the couch with my back to the window. At full capacity, twelve of us would squeeze into Barb's cozy office, transformed into a circle with the addition of her dining room chairs, reminding me of my years facilitating group meetings. After ten minutes or so of discussion about social or political issues about which we all passionately agreed, Marni would say, "Okay, who has work for today?" and we'd be off and running. On Thursdays at Barb's, I felt like a little kid at story hour listening to their wonderful writing. If it was my week, I found I was anxious to read and get it over with, but also eager to get feedback and help. I would return to my condo after our sessions, hungry for my lunch, but even hungrier to read the comments and suggestions on the printed copies I'd handed out. When I saw a scribbled heart or a "love this," I'd feel great. But, even more, I came to love the suggestions for alternate word choices or ways to say or do something. In the beginning, the comments were just encouraging, but over time, they became more constructive: "You could skip all this," or "Put this here," or "Elaborate on this."

Being a member of The Feisty Writers became my weekly touchstone as a single woman living alone. Our meeting was, and still is, one of the few recurring weekly events on my calendar. My fellow Feisties have been patient and supportive, encouraging and helpful. They critique with brilliance but also cheer each other on and celebrate publishing milestones with champagne. We have become more than a writing group; we are a community of women: open, honest, and vulnerable. We are courageous storytellers and caring, extraordinary people. Finding this group at this time in my life provided me with an optimal frame of support as I worked on my memoir.

As I turned eighty, I was content and engaged; I loved the writing and the writing group. I certainly wasn't expecting anything new and surprising of a positive nature, but . . .

# PART V

———

## My 80s Plus
## CELEBRATING

# SURPRISE! SURPRISE!

July 2016

Six months after my eightieth birthday, I stood relaxing in my kitchen, pouring my five o'clock glass of sauvignon blanc while chatting with my daughter Donna and grandson Kai. Jeremy and Julian had left that morning to take Julian to a music camp in the Midwest, but Donna and Kai were staying for another week. We were beginning to discuss our plans for dinner when the phone rang. The answering machine announced *Spector*, so I picked up the receiver, thinking it was Wendy or Sharrin. But the announcement continued: *Jonah*. I scanned the Spector file in my head. *Was there a Jonah Spector? Maybe some long-lost cousin of my ex-husband Myles?*

I answered the phone with a question mark. "Hello?"

It was a male voice with a New York accent. "Hello?" also with a question mark. And then, "Wait, you're not my ex-wife, Suzy."

"No," I laughed. "This is the other Suzy Spector."

"What!" he exclaimed. "There are *two* of you?"

"Yes. And, not only that, we both used to live in Solana Beach, and now we're both in Encinitas."

"How do you know that?" he asked, incredulously.

As I walked into the front room to privately continue the conversation, Donna called out a warning, "Mom, stop giving away your identity." I shrugged her off, thinking, *Don't be paranoid. I know this man. He's New York Jewish.*

I closed the front room doors and continued. "Well, thirty-four years ago, my furniture arrived in Solana Beach from New York without a warning, and I said to the moving man, 'How could you just show up without calling me first?'

"He replied, 'Lady, I did call, and your son said it was okay to make the delivery.'

"'Guess what?' I told him, 'I don't have a son.'

"'Well, Madam,' he told me, 'there's somebody named Suzanne Spector in the Solana Beach phone book who has a son.'

"So," I said to Jonah, "I guess that was *your* son. But how come you called *my* number? Don't you know your ex-wife's phone number?"

"No, we've been divorced for over thirty years. I needed my grandson's new address so I could send him a birthday check." Jonah continued, "Did you know the other Suzy Spector is a terrific artist?"

"I thought you were the artist."

"Me!" he exclaimed. "What do you know about me?"

"Well, I lived in Solana Beach for ten years, and every place I went they asked, 'Spector? Are you from Spector Design?' I assume that was your business."

"It was. I wrote a story about that. It's in my memoir. If you want to give me your email address, I'll send you the story."

As I recited my email address, Donna and Kai shouted in unison from the other room, "Mom! Nana!—your identity! Stop giving it away."

So much for privacy! I had put those doors on the room years before to create a sense of privacy for my clients when I used the room as a therapy office. I forgot that the doors weren't soundproof—I'd lived alone there for a quarter century.

At dinner I found my mind wandering occasionally. I was intrigued that Jonah had written his memoir. As soon as we returned home, I checked my iPad. *Just curious*, I said to myself. Sure enough, Jonah had already sent me an email. And thus, it began.

We emailed so much that I became conditioned to the happy ping of *You've Got Mail*. After two weeks, he said, "We must meet. How about tomorrow for lunch?"

I told myself I was totally "cool" about getting together, but I tried on my entire summer maxi dress collection that night before our date. I knew he liked bright colors based on a photo he'd sent of his twenty pairs of colored sneakers. I chose my loudest dress—a bright orchid, sleeveless sheath, with all my lumps, bumps, and wrinkles on full display.

Even though I told myself it was just a casual meeting between two New York Jewish transplants, I arrived at Fidel's flustered and five minutes late. I saw him waiting in the entryway, and distracted by his bright orange T-shirt, I scraped my fender as I pulled into a spot. *Should we have stuck to email?*

But as we settled into a booth and started munching on chips and salsa, I relaxed. The aboriginal art that covered the front of his shirt was a conversation starter. We talked about travels and art and New York bagels, about children and grandchildren, writing and tennis. He told me a sexual fantasy, and I told him one back. *Did I really do that?* We talked non-stop for almost three hours. Then out of nowhere, he leaned forward and said, "I'd like to kiss you right now."

Without skipping a beat, I replied, "I'm really enjoying our connection, but I have to confess that my hormones aren't working anymore. They sure drove me when I was younger, but now they're gone."

My disclaimer wasn't a deal breaker. We kept on talking. When we finally got up from the table to leave, he put his arm around me and gave me a little hug. It felt delicious. As I leaned into it, I thought, *Hmm, what's this about? I didn't know I had any juice left.*

———

He began signing his emails "love." I wasn't going there, so I signed mine with a yellow heart emoji. I'd never used emojis before, but they sure were handy. When he asked what the yellow heart meant, I said, "Not stop or go, just yellow. But a heart."

I was enjoying this email flirtation. I had stopped dating so long ago, I don't think the Internet existed back then. I could remember reading and placing ads in the personals section of the *San Diego Reader*. What duds that turned up! I had been happy to give up sex and settle into my deep friendship with Robert, but he had been dead for six years now. When Jonah asked me to suggest a place for our first lunch date, I'd thought of Fidel's; it was where I'd had my first lunch date with Robert years before.

Sexual overtures were made online by Jonah and ignored by me. But, on our third lunch date, he leaned across the café table on Cedros and stunned me by saying, "I've never met a woman like you. I think about you all the time. And I don't understand the mixed signals you're giving by pulling away physically." Before I could sputter a reply, he continued, "I love you, and I don't understand why you're being so skittish about making love. At our age, we don't have time to waste."

"Well," I answered, "I'm afraid if we started to share more physical closeness, you'd just be coming over, and we wouldn't be leaving the house much. I like to get out and do stuff."

He looked at me in disbelief. "We have so much in common, how could you possibly think it would only be one thing?" I thought, *Oh my God. Is this really happening?*

I came home feeling floaty and warm. *This might be fun. I like this man.* I decided to send him the heart emojis in every color without saying anything. I opened my iPad, took a deep breath, and instead, I hit the vibrating heart emoji. To me that said, "My heart is pounding." Then I wrote, "Okay, carpe diem," and signed it with the emoji of two dancing hearts. As I pushed the send button, my stomach flipped. I had dived in. I was scared and excited. I felt the walls protecting my self-sufficiency beginning to melt. After forty-plus years as a happy single woman, could I open myself to be loved?

Six weeks after the wrong number phone call, we made love for the first time. It was marvelous. He was open, at ease, and loving. I was too. We were both so thrilled to have found each other, to be enjoying sex with each other, in whatever forms it took, including sometimes simply cuddling up on the bed, touching, and being close. I was delighted that I was not self-conscious about my eighty-year-old body. We laughed a lot as we sought comfortable positions for our aged joints. I felt my second chakra ignite and actually pulsate; I thought that spigot had dried up years ago. Was there an emoji for that?

After a couple of hours of loving closeness and pleasure, we took a bagel break. Then we went back upstairs for more. Jonah had us look in the mirror together, admiring how wonderful we looked as a couple. He thought I was beautiful, even with my clothes off.

I never expected to connect so deeply with a man, and at age eighty. What I really didn't see coming was that the sex got hotter and hotter. He introduced me to my G spot and other previously unexplored sources of pleasure as well. Orgasms were not the old one-big-shot-and-it's-over variety. The passionate pleasure we shared was charged and continuous, like the dancing hearts emoji.

When we first met, Jonah moved to the Gaslamp neighborhood of downtown San Diego, and we had a good time exploring the urban vibe together. After all my years of singlehood, I enjoyed having a dinner companion several nights a week and the novelty of sharing shopping and mundane chores. But I also liked my daily beach walks, writing, and alone time with my family, friends, and women's circles. I hungered for more spaciousness and solitude. Over time, despite the marvelous sexual connection, my independence became a source of too much friction between us, and we split up. I wished for him to find a full-time companion, and for me to regain my footing as captain of my own ship. The possibility of a love connection and sexual adventure was fun to explore at eighty, and I have no regrets. It was a great experience. He has a new girlfriend, and I have my life back and my own rhythm. We are fond friends now and enjoy catching up regularly . . . on the telephone. Once again, I expected no more surprises, and then . . .

# TAKING A BOW

Spring 2019

I intended to end this memoir on my eightieth birthday in January of 2016. Then Jonah entered my life, and that "wrong number" story just begged to be told; it was a fitting bookend to the story of my leap out of my marriage onto nude beaches in La Jolla, Greece, and Ibiza forty years earlier.

But I have one more story to tell—a final leap for me, another experience beyond my wildest dreams. I had a single-minded focus on finishing this book, but when the theme of the Fifth Annual Memoir Showcase competition in San Diego was announced, I experienced one of those body rushes, like I've had preceding other leaps in my life. The 2019 showcase theme was "I Didn't See That One Coming," and my inner voice screamed, *You must stop working on your memoir and write an entry about your relationship with Jonah!*

My story, "Dancing Hearts Emoji," was one of ten selected out of almost two hundred entries to be performed on stage by professional actors at the North Coast Repertory Theatre in October of 2019 and to be published in the anthology

*Shaking the Tree*, Volume 3. At the showcase performance a year earlier, I had helped serve wine in the theater lobby. A year later, I felt like a grown-up at the writers' table, seated in the audience, surrounded by The Feisties, who had encouraged me from the beginning and helped me polish my entry.

The actress who read my piece captured our accents, our banter, and the nuances of our relationship, and she looked better in her slim maxi dress then I ever had in mine. Yet the entire time she read my piece, I sat in the audience, and I blushed. Forty-plus years of stripping away old conditioning about women's sexuality, and I still blushed. From my 700-page original autobiography to this memoir, my sexuality, or really my life force, emerged as the brightest thread, the story that needed to be told. Yet here I was, taking one last leap, and what did I do? I blushed.

My generation did not talk about sex. I want to get over my embarrassment and tell my story, to contribute to shedding light on women's sexuality, one story at a time, one set of wiring and hormones and culture at a time. I'm not saying other women should be like me, but I hope my truth will inspire others to accept themselves, live their truth, and maybe understand a little better why they did or didn't do certain things on their life journey, as other women's truth-telling helps me understand and claim mine. If young women can come forth in the #MeToo movement, the least I'd like to do is tell my story without blushing. This is a goal I'm still working on.

I've learned so much from The Feisty Writers and the Tree Goddesses, and it hasn't only been about writing. As I listen to these brilliant, beautiful young women, mostly in their fifties and sixties, a few with mothers my age or even a little older, I realize I may be more of a realistic role model of what their aging and old age can be than the images they hold of their mothers and grandmothers.

Although I blushed that night in the theater, I was proud to hear the laughter and applause and to get up on stage afterward alongside the other writers and actors and take a bow. Mine is not a "they lived happily ever after" story, it's a "she had the courage to live fully and be the creator of her own life" story.

I wonder what's next.

# ACKNOWLEDGMENTS

The title of my memoir reflects my desire, in the second half of my life, to be the captain of my own ship rather than coupled. However, one of the takeaways of this journey, both in life and on the page, is that I was not alone because I was engaged in myriad wonderful relationships and experiences. I'd like to thank all the "characters" in this book, whether in my life for a month, a year, or much longer. You are mentioned because you were a significant teacher, support, guide, companion, or all that and more to me on my journey. To those who read these pages and find that I omitted our connection, please understand that the structure of memoir limits me to certain themes. Cherished but somehow not mentioned? My best friend from high school and first adventure partner, Sue Coan; my other New York "Ya-Yas" Barbara Azzara and Renee Landau; also, my oldest San Diego buddy, Elsie Zala, who is now ninety-six and may well outlive me. I have been so fortunate to manifest such an extraordinary sisterhood in my adult life.

At age eighty-six, I share love, understanding, and support in four different circles of women here in San Diego. For thirty years I have met once a month to meditate, celebrate, and eat with Anna Benson, Pat Bryning, Judy Ervice, Judith Matson, and Livia Walsh. We named ourselves Creative Women. We never manifested artistic creativity, but we supported each other as we each created our own life path. In Chapter 30, I wrote about the art and soul journey I began in my seventies, led by Laura Hansen. Together with fellow

"Soul Sisters" Althea Brimm, Marla English, Judy Ervice, Suzanna Neal, and Livia Walsh, we still gather monthly to do readings from our SoulCollage cards. Even over Zoom, we go to a profound place of understanding and support together. My heart is joined and my roots deeply intertwined with those of my dear Tree Sisters: Elizabeth Eshoo, Laura Hansen, Chris Lehman, Wendy Shaw, and Wendy Wolff, inspired in our journaling process by Lois Sunrich.

I thank the extraordinary women who have supported me and guided my life as a writer. Lois Sunrich fanned the flames of my writing interest with perfect prompts, then patiently listened as I spilled out my story on page after page; then she kicked me out of the nest and insisted I was ready to go off to school to learn the craft. At San Diego Writers, Ink, I met Marni Freedman, who became my writing coach and "book mama." Marni nurtured me with patience and brilliance privately and within her extraordinary circle of talented women, The Feisty Writers. Eight pages at a time, they encouraged me through the writing of what eventually became a 700-page, two-volume autobiography. The Feisties' responses to my life stories inspired me to shift my purpose from an autobiographical record for my family to a memoir for other women who are navigating the second half of life. My thanks to Tracy Jones for her role in my transition from autobiography to memoir.

I have appreciated the support and encouragement, guidance, and skill of each of my Feisty Writer sisters, both past and present. Mentioning the names in our Feisty family—Phyllis Olins, Kimberly Pierce, Tania Pryputniewicz, Nicola Ranson, Lindsey Salatka, Gina Simmons, Barbara Thompson, and Anastasia Hipkins—does not begin to capture the love I feel for these women and the gratitude I have for their central role in my life these last six years. I would like to especially acknowledge Donna Agins for her friendship, hand-holding, and coaching throughout the entire journey.

Elizabeth Eshoo is the midwife of this memoir; she helped me find the book I wanted to write and guided me all the way from conception to delivery of a completed manuscript. For that first big step out of the Feisty family, I had three marvelous beta readers: Laura Hansen, Nancy Johnson, and Wendy Woolf. Their editing was extraordinary, incisive, and invaluable.

For the last phase and final polish, Marni Freedman, Lindsey Salatka, and Anastasia Hipkins came back in with incredible editorial talent and support. Jen Laffler, who had helped and encouraged me all along, became my alter ego, voice, eyes, and support for pre-publication tasks and social media. Finally, sincerest thanks to my publishing team. As soon as I heard about She Writes Press, I knew that's where I wanted to land. I love their model—a nurturing, inspiring community of women writers—and I love the quality of their product. Thank you, Brooke Warner, and all who work at She Writes. I was thrilled to be accepted into the family and value my fellow writers on the She Writes path.

And last, but always first whether they felt it or not, my gratitude goes to my three extraordinary daughters, Wendy Spector, Donna Anderson, and Sharrin Spector. I have respected your wishes by not writing about you in this memoir, except for the milestones we celebrated together. You already know: you are my heart-song.

# ABOUT THE AUTHOR

Photo credit: Michele Goane

SUZANNE SPECTOR is a graduate of Barnard College and holds a master's degree from the Columbia University School of Social Work. She was Coordinator of the American Montessori Teacher Training Program, then founded and directed The Center for Open Education, an innovative school, before becoming the Director of the Center for Studies of the Person. At age fifty-six, she earned her PhD from The Union Institute. At age seventy-seven, she began to write. Her essays *My Path to CSP* and *A Deeper Listening* were published in the anthology *A Place to Be: CSP at Fifty (2017)*. Her short story *Dancing Heart Emoji* won the 2019 SDMWA Memoir Showcase Award and was published in *Shaking the Tree: Volume Three (2021)*. *Naked at the Helm* was accepted for publication by She Writes Press when Suzanne was eighty-five years old.

# BOOK CLUB GUIDE

1. What do you think the author meant by the title *Naked at the Helm*? What does it mean to you?

2. What was your favorite chapter of the book? Why?

3. If you were to title the chapter of your life you are in right now, what might it be?

4. Do you ever feel lost, paralyzed, or stuck, wondering, *Who am I?*

5. The author jumps into new experiences and discovers herself (e.g., leaving her secure New York life and moving to California, where she has no friends and no job). Have you ever leaped into the unknown? Where did it lead you?

6. The author's "soul place" is walking along the ocean's edge. What's yours?

7. The author finds an element of freedom in talking about sexuality with her best friend. Do you talk about sexuality with your best friend? Your partner? In groups? In public?

8. The value of women's friendship is an important theme in this memoir. How do you think this relates to the author not having a primary partner in the second half of her life?

9. Looking back on your life so far, what is the biggest risk you have taken? Are you glad you did?

10. Looking forward, what is something you would like to do? What steps could you take to make that happen?

# ART PROJECT: LIFE COLLAGE

You learned in *Naked at the Helm* that the author began to explore art as a means of self-expression in her sixties. Here is an easy art project to do with your book club or on your own.

To do this collage you will need these supplies:

1. 11x14 heavyweight paper. Cardboard or artboard is a good choice here.
2. Scissors
3. Magazines with photos of people, places and interesting objects
4. Glue sticks
5. Magic markers

Before you begin the project, do a five-minute meditation. (It would be wise to set a timer.)

1. Sit with your eyes closed, feet on the floor, and hands resting on your lap.
2. Focus on following your breath: inhale and exhale, in and out. If your mind wanders, refocus on your breath.
3. When the alarm rings, open your eyes and choose one of the following prompts:

    - How would you portray this chapter of your life?
    - Where is your soul place?
    - What life leap would you like to take?

## Life Collage

Create a Life Collage based on one of the above prompts or a question of your own prompted by your reaction to the book.

1. Sort through pictures from magazines and photos you have on hand.
2. Cut out or tear out pictures, words and phrases that illustrate your response to the prompt.
3. Arrange them on the 11x14 paper in a way that makes sense to you. There are no wrong answers.
4. Once you have your photos in place, glue them onto your board.
5. When you are finished gluing, you can use markers to label or emphasize one or more photos and phrases. You may also want to add a saying or draw patterns to enhance your Life Collage.

## Sharing

If you've done this project in a group, sit in a circle and, if you want, take turns sharing your Life Collages and what you were each hoping to express. Refrain from judgmental comments about each other's collages. Did this process make you feel more "naked at the helm"? Discuss with the group.

## SELECTED TITLES FROM SHE WRITES PRESS

She Writes Press is an independent publishing company
founded to serve women writers everywhere.
Visit us at www.shewritespress.com.

*A Delightful Little Book on Aging* by Stephanie Raffelock. $19.95, 978-1-63152-840-8. A collection of thoughts and stories woven together with a fresh philosophy that helps to dispel some of the toxic stereotypes of aging, this inspirational, empowering, and emotionally honest look at life's journey is part joyful celebration and part invitation to readers to live life fully to the very end.

*The Book of Old Ladies: Celebrating Women of a Certain Age in Fiction* by Ruth O. Saxton. $16.95, 978-1-63152-797-5. In this book lover's guide to approaching old age and its losses while still embracing beauty, sensuality, creativity, connection, wonder, and joy, Ruth Saxton introduces readers to thirty modern stories featuring "women of a certain age" who prepare for the journey of aging, inhabit the territory, and increasingly become their truest selves.

*Flip-Flops After Fifty: And Other Thoughts on Aging I Remembered to Write Down* by Cindy Eastman. $16.95, 978-1-93831-468-1. A collection of frank and funny essays about turning fifty—and all the emotional ups and downs that come with it.

*Brave(ish): A Memoir of a Recovering Perfectionist* by Margaret Davis Ghielmetti. $16.95, 978-1-63152-747-0. An intrepid traveler sets off at forty to live the expatriate dream overseas—only to discover that she has no idea how to live even her own life. Part travelogue and part transformation tale, Ghielmetti's memoir, narrated with humor and warmth, proves that it's never too late to reconnect with our authentic selves—if we dare to put our own lives first at last.

*Operatic Divas and Naked Irishmen: An Innkeeper's Tale* by Nancy R. Hinchliff. $16.95, 978-1-63152-194-2. At sixty four, divorced, retired, and with no prior business experience and little start-up money, Nancy Hinchliff impulsively moves to a new city where she knows only one person, buys a 125-year-old historic mansion, and turns it into a bed and breakfast.